Live

2

not what i am

the experience of performing

interviews by david tushingham

photographs by simon annand

Methuen Drama

First published in Great Britain in 1995 by Methuen Drama

ISBN 0 413 69010 5
A CIP catalogue record for this book
is available at the British Library

Typeset by Deltatype Ltd, Ellesmere Port, Cheshire

contents

The ground upon which any aesthetic debate in the theatre will be carried out lies not in the writer's study, the director's office or the rehearsal room, but in that strange collision between the worlds on and off stage, between the performers and the audience.

What actually happens during this process can be highly elusive. The experience of performing is a topic many performers are reluctant to discuss in public because they are called upon to generalise about something which is always particular. To do so would be to risk being pretentious or boring or untrue to themselves – everything they have devoted their lives to avoiding on stage.

Yet talk about it we must – and do. Because it's fun. There's a personal need to reconsider the last performance and look forward to the next. Rehearsal rooms, dressing rooms, green rooms, bars – all spaces immediately adjacent to scenes of live performance – are favourite locations for what over time becomes a single, highly infectious and apparently never-ending discussion.

This discussion is endless because it is part of a lively, ongoing tradition. The interviews in this volume will never answer all the questions which the experience of performing raises. What they can do is present today's answers to today's questions. We offer them to you in the knowledge that for the contributors they represent the latest step in their own tireless search for better, more compelling, more fulfilling theatre, a search which will go on beyond this volume.

Special thanks are due to Sue Higginson and the staff of the Royal National Theatre Studio for their continued help and support during this project.

simon callow
Who the fuck are we?

Simon Callow is an actor, writer and director. He trained at
the Drama Centre and spent much of the seventies acting
with fringe companies such as Joint Stock and the Bush
before joining the National Theatre, where he created the
role of Mozart in the original production of Peter Shaffer's
Amadeus. *Being an Actor*, published in 1984, has since
acquired the status of a classic. He has recently published a
biography of Orson Welles.

My first experiences of theatre are what I've always taken as the lodestone of my own aspirations as an actor and what I would like to create in the actors that I work with as a director. I managed to catch the last flourish of an absolutely extraordinary generation of actors, that is Edith Evans, Sybil Thorndike, Gielgud, Olivier, Richardson and among foreign actors Eduardo De Filippo – who I think probably was the most extraordinary single actor that I've ever seen – Anna Magnani . . . Michael Redgrave, Peggy Ashcroft: this great swathe of remarkable actors, remarkable artists, remarkable personalities. Though many of them had acted in films, they were above all stage actors and they had their training and their whole being in the theatre.

I have always believed the theatre, of its nature, demands a certain scale. It's a mythical medium, a mythifying medium, and it needs to aspire towards that. It's not a naturalistic medium. It's not a medium of verisimilitude, it's one of **intensification**. It's a heightened art form. Although our theatre isn't quite as conventional as Kabuki or Noh theatre, nonetheless that's the sort of area in which it works.

Do you have an ideal theatre or a favourite theatre – in architectural terms, size and shape?

A theatre that I loved deeply, which was duly sort of destroyed by developers, was the original Mermaid Theatre of Bernard Miles. Although – this is more sentimental than anything else – the Old Vic in Olivier's time was also for me the prototypical playhouse because it was where the greatest magic, the most potent spectacles occurred. What Olivier and Sean Kenny between them did to the theatre was to tone it down so that funnily enough the auditorium became rather dull, sombre colours; and they basically took away the proscenium. That had a tremendous focus on the stage.

It's very interesting that when the Mirvishes so very kindly renovated it and restored it to all its Victorian glory, they actually somehow managed to demolish the ghosts at the same time. Nowadays you really do have a frame, like a photograph frame, you stick the photograph in and it's got this nice, embellished frame. But I'm afraid for me, though I've worked there lately with *Carmen Jones*, the theatre has none of the rough power of Olivier's theatre.

It's interesting that it was like that, because I only know the Old Vic in its present incarnation and it does somehow to me feel a little sterile, resisting all my efforts to imagine those great productions happening there.

It was a very extraordinary time when that company was exploring the world repertory under the tutelage of various extraordinary directors, like Jacques Charon or designers like Josef Svoboda and so on. The National Theatre has become very parochial by comparison with those days. Even though there are certain admired avant-gardists like Robert Lepage who drop in, it's very hard to create the excitement that Olivier had. Because he was making a company. You can't have that sense of excitement: as actors begin to find themselves and become extraordinary before our very eyes.

And there isn't that sense that the theatre really belongs to the actors who perform there.

Very much so. It really did feel like that. Of course the bigger the theatre, the harder that is to achieve and the more auditoria there are, the harder it is to achieve. When a theatre becomes an empire, then you're in trouble.

In *Being an Actor*, you quote Vakhtangov: 'To act is to want, to want and to want again.' I wondered whether and how one's wants as an actor change.

Of course, he was almost outlining a technical notion which is that in the Stanislavskian sense every thing that happens on the stage must be an action – in other words it must be towards getting something. The more you want that thing and the greater the obstacle, the greater the effort will be. It's a brilliantly chosen phrase because we have to develop it like an appetite, a need for things. The trouble with that is it's a very vulnerable thing to do, to want things very much. It's often not an accident that the most ambitious actors often turn out to be in a sense the best – because they know what wanting is all about. They **want** to be famous – or whatever. My teachers used to say it really doesn't matter **what** you want, just cultivate the appetite that you have – don't stand away from it, stand over it.

You can see an actor like Laughton is wonderfully full of wants.

'Want' is also a very good word to use because – God knows what it was in Russian – because of 'to want' in its other sense, to find something wanting, lacking something.

There's something missing that you're wanting to complete.

Exactly. What I have observed a great, great deal – there are many things one observes about the development of modern acting, the changes that have occurred – but it's curiously lacking in urgency or indeed in personal identification. What I'm particularly aware of is actors playing lightly, quite deftly, skilfully but in a curiously impersonal sort of way. And it's to do with not wanting to reveal the want. I think that's fashion. I think it came to seem to be rather old-fashioned, rather vulgar, rather crass, a rather gross thing to really show yourself quite so much.

Olivier was naked, that was the extraordinary thing. Of course Olivier had the technical armoury which no one who has ever acted has ever had and no one ever will have again. He worked on his own puny little body to such an extent and his own miserable little voice to such an extraordinary degree that it reminds me of a wonderful film by Herzog called *The Great Ecstasy of Woodcarver Steiner*. It's about a chap who's the greatest skier in the world, he's the absolute emperor of the piste, and they've actually had to ban him because he's so far ahead of everybody else that he makes the competition pointless, he's entered into it so completely. That is true of Olivier.

I'm talking about technique now, I'm not talking about interpretation or the art. In many ways Olivier was a very crude artist and in many ways he wasn't an artist at all but as a kind of technician it was just unbelievable what he did. In a funny way I found that touching, because you saw him amassing this fabulous technique and displaying it glitteringly and his desire for your admiration, his desire for your approval, was so charming to me, I gave in instantly. Many people resisted it violently and said: Why am I being coerced? Why is there a pistol being held up to my head? But I always saw the puny little boy inside Olivier and that always moved me terribly.

I'm talking about a man who's living out his own personal drama on a rather massive scale – to me that's pretty well what artists are supposed to do, whether they're painters or novelists or sculptors, it's: Here I am. But you see I'm using words that are deemed to be a bit inappropriate nowadays. I'm saying 'artist' and it's not something actors generally like to say about themselves any more.

In fact I believe that actors have rather abandoned a concept of themselves at all. When they're challenged to say: Well, what is this that you do? What kind of creature are you?, they all make embarrassed denials, they take refuge in saying: Well, you know, I just, you know, do a job and that's it. I learn the lines and don't bump into the furniture and that's all there is to it. I understand why people say that – perhaps because it's true. But I think that it's something else. I think it's a vocation.

Many, many years ago when Adrian Noble and I worked together on *Titus Andronicus* it was the first Shakespeare play that either of us had ever done and Adrian just said to me – I don't remember why – but he said to me: Why do you act? And I said, without a moment's hesitation: Because it is in my nature to do so. And that's something that I think is very important about acting. It's actually something that I haven't done very much lately, I haven't acted full out for a long, long time. The last time I did that was when I acted in *Faust* at the Lyric, Hammersmith, and that was so unsatisfactory as a production and so inferior as a performance that I'm embarrassed by it, frankly. It's a long time since I've really done the works, last time I did that was *Kiss of the Spiderwoman*. And if you were to ask me: Out of all the acting performances you've given what is the one that would suggest, **suggest** what you think acting is about, I would say: That, even though it was by no means perfect. I gave in to it completely and did, I know, fulfil it completely to the uttermost of my own being.

I was brought up as a Catholic. Somewhere in the back of my mind is some sort of religious notion of acting and I know it belongs to my days as an altar servant. In the Catholic Church – I suppose in the Anglican Church too – there's a vestry where the priest puts on his garments. It's one of the most vivid memories of my life, making jokes with the priest, specially the kind of priests they were, Irish Christian Brothers, full of sly jibs and jibes. It was all very funny and then we'd go into the vestry and then they'd start to robe and to garb themselves and then they became someone else. And they walked out up to that altar vested in every sense with a power which made them more than who they were. And that is an idea that I have about acting – that idea is that you function at a higher level as an actor.

I'm sure everybody would agree with that, but nobody really worries about how to take the steps to make that happen. I think it's partly to do with actors' conceptions of themselves, the way that they see themselves. I think we're a bit lost at this point in history as to who the fuck we are. There are one or two people, like Steven Berkoff for example, who has no doubts as to who the fuck he is, but Steven just happens to function in a very, very stylised area. It's remarkable and I admire him intensely – I think his work on himself has been quite, quite exceptional – but he's confined himself deliberately to a very limited area of expression.

I think it's interesting the role that the Poor Theatre idea has played in all of this. Because I think originally it grew out of a real – and certainly in the case of Grotowski a very religious – belief in the power of acting, how incredible it could be. It didn't actually need all this paraphernalia of set and costumes and effects. And somehow for a whole generation of people who have grown up with this view it's led to a distrust of all forms of spectacle.

The problem with Grotowski for me has always been that he has no sense of play in performance and there is a line in that book which says: Laughter is banned from our rehearsals. That's when I stopped reading the book because I knew that – I don't think these things are actually opposed to each other and they in fact deliberately belong in dialectical harness – the other critical aspect of acting is its **liberation**. It must be a liberation. And that's again where you get the most extraordinary performances from actors who find their liberation through a character, the relief of not being themselves, the joy of playing, having a life inside them which has its own rules, its organic kind of shape, which is not subject to the negotiations, the compromises and the disappointments of life.

It's a critical, critical thing and that's what actors and actresses have said through the ages – you know Arkadina in *The Seagull* says: I wish I was in a nice poor hotel room, just learning my part – I could become more complete, more fulfilled. I subscribe to that view very much and I know that that's something which is rather frowned on too. But rarely do I see on the stage nowadays actors who seem to me to have been acting out their own lives – I don't mean in a realistic or documentary sense – I don't get the rush that comes from the freedom that the mask gives.

And being able to find a part of their life on stage that they might not have access to off stage?

And that's a very naked thing to do or to admit to. But it's just a fact you've got to live with. I've complicated my own life in many ways and one of them is because I do writing and directing as well but also I haven't dedicated myself to acting as I probably should have done. I did a play in Leicester last year, I directed it and acted in it. Only on the last night of the run did I remember why I was an actor at all in the first place, I was so concerned to serve the play, so concerned with all the other aspects of the production that it wasn't literally until the three last days, the three last performances, that I suddenly remembered that being an actor is about **celebrating**, always celebrating the whole human condition. Whatever aspect of it you're illuminating, that's the job.

Daunting thought, isn't it? Especially if you're in a run of a year, or you're doing four plays at the RSC, you think: Fucking hell, I've got to stand up on stage and celebrate the fucking human condition. Well, that's unfortunate – if you're conducting Bruckner's Eighth Symphony, you'd better really pay homage, tribute to the universal struggle that that man chose to put into his music. You've got to live it as if he was just writing it.

Now I personally think that in our theatres there's an absence of methodology and I accuse myself of that more than anyone and that's where I'd like to reassess my approach to acting. As an actor I've always been rather intuitive but I think sometimes with a following wind my intuition has not misled me. As a director I find that I'm perfectly intelligent and intelligible, I think interpretatively I'm quite sound. Sometimes I've managed to reach to the heart of an actor and say the right thing which will enable them to throw off their shackles. But there's another way, there's a more methodical way of achieving this.

The most remarkable thing I've seen in the theatre recently, the thing which actually reduced me utterly to tears for the whole length of the production, was Lev Dodin's production of *The Cherry Orchard*. I'm not certain by any means that Dodin's interpretation of *The Cherry Orchard* is ideal, I'm not even sure to be honest that some of the actors were terribly well cast in their parts; what I am absolutely sure about is that there was a richer poetic connection with human life, with genuine human values than I have seen for many, many, many a year and it's not at all surprising to learn that Dodin has worked with the same actors for many, many years. They came out of his school, they work with a very well-structured approach that he has devised with them over the years and they rehearse for weeks and months and years, sometimes.

The commitment of the actors to that approach was so heart-rending. To see the party guests – it's a company of fifty so they could afford this kind of splendour – but the leading actors from other plays were the party guests in the third act and every single one of them had a life of such richness and intensity: **centred**, not externally applied. There's a tremendous amount of external application of detail which is not the same thing as character. That's characteristics, it's not character, that's not grasping the central principle of another human life and installing it in your own self.

This idea, this centredness, is very critical to me. It's getting hold of the main thing. Before you start embellishing, get the ABC, get the fundamentals. Lately I've seen a lot of productions that are acclaimed as radical reconceptions of plays. What they actually are is rehearsal exercises. They explore an element of the play, an aspect of it. This is then elevated into a whole production.

It becomes a concept.

That's right. And that sort of partial quality, the peculiar sense that one has so, so often in theatre now that you've not got the whole thing, you've got a sort of **fraction**. And it's not because people aren't working hard, it's not because they aren't serious about what they're doing and intelligent and all the rest of it. It's because everything is commentary now. Nothing is reality.

Edith Evans – when you think back over the famous performances which she gave, her Restoration characters and her Cleopatra and so on and so forth, I don't think anybody would think or did think at the time of talking about her **interpretation**. I don't think that even crossed their minds.

They didn't say: Ah, now her angle on Cleopatra is . . . Not at all. All she did was to fill herself with Cleopatra and then irradiate it again. The concept that you have to reach this strange area where you're talking about yourself as much as the character, it's a very hard area.

I think that's very interesting because one of the things I find terribly attractive about particularly those great plays is that I don't think it's possible to see a *Hamlet* which will make you never want to see *Hamlet* again, to see a *Cherry Orchard* or a *Three Sisters* which will make you never want to see those plays—

A final statement.

And you'll never get all of them – you'll get certain things and you won't get others. And it was interesting for me what you said about Olivier, that he was tremendously strong at doing particular things and that if you wanted to find them there were weaknesses as well – but that somehow these weaknesses made the performance for you more attractive. And I think that's actually one of the perennial fascinations of these works of art. They are complex matrices of interactions between whole groups of people. So you can have historically significant productions but I don't think you'll ever have a production which abolishes everything else – which I think is very encouraging.

Orson Welles has a very peculiar remark, he said, 'Actors are a third sex. They're neither masculine nor feminine. They're a third sex. They're another breed. They're something different and separate from the rest of mankind. It's a strange, peculiar, maybe even perverted kind of profession.' And it is a weird old job. Being out there is a very, very specialised way of being. You have to cultivate it. It's no good just saying: That's what I do, I'm this sort of person and then at five to seven I get to the theatre and at half past seven I'm King Lear. Michael Redgrave said that if you do play one of those great parts you wake up and the first thing that comes into your mind is: Performance tonight.

It's not just will you be able to accomplish it physically, but that you have to start opening the sluicegates of your own psyche or whatever other less portentous word we can find for it, the psychological elements of oneself, to be ready and tuned. And there are people – people I know – who actually find acting an immoral job because it involves you in creating, recreating and reproducing an emotion which you yourself in real life are not feeling at that moment. It's like some extraordinary kind of prostitution. And I have some sympathy with that view, but I'm afraid that's the way I'm made.

Do think that acting is something in which it's possible to progress, that it's possible to learn from what previous generations have done and add additional refinements? Is it a body of knowledge which can be added to – or more of a constant struggle which has to be waged?

Well I think progress is possible. But the tradition has been different. It has been that every generation reacts against the generation of its predecessors. So Olivier, for example – rather surprisingly, we would think, but it's true – Olivier was rejecting the noble, sonorous, lyrical and generalised acting of the generation before him. He was rooting everything in psychological reference points. He said: Iago is about stripes, that's what it's about. He didn't talk about embodying or finding the medieval devil figure, you know, he wasn't interested in any of that or any kind of general embodiment of evil. What he wanted to do was to make the audience think: I know a man like that! It was what one of his critics called the shock of recognition. That was his innovation. And his other innovations were rhythmic. He created extraordinary jagged rhythms, attention-getting moments, and instead of a mellifluousness of tone what he cultivated was contrast.

Now, there was a big reaction against this. Everybody said: No, no, no, it's showy-offy, it looks like acting. I can see the wheels going round, everyone used to say, as if they'd just thought of the phrase. They all said it. Everybody said it – and that was his whole point. I think he said that he wanted to fascinate the public with the art of acting, so he did, you know. All this dazzlement and what will he do next? And very often at the cost, it must be said, of the natural line of the role. Olivier was always surprising.

Now, a new generation came along and every generation of actors tries to give the audience something new and in a sense to say: No, no, no, that isn't what acting is, **this** is what acting is. And of course the generation after Olivier said good acting is about reality, documentary reality. So you had the generation of Albert Finney, Alan Bates and so on, basically they were saying, you know, it was the message of the Royal Court: truth and social realism was what they wanted.

What happened then is a little harder to put your finger on because unfortunately actors like Albert Finney and Alan Bates didn't quite take on the mantle. For some reason they didn't accept that. Their triumphs have been mainly on celluloid. But anyway, what happened subsequently was the next generation of actors – I suppose I'm part of the next generation of actors – there we were, we were really in a kind of void and we were working on the fringe and so on. Basically our acting, actually most of my generation, was an attempt to reclaim some of the theatrical ground, I think. I think you'll see in the work of actors like Tony Sher or myself an attempt to sort of instil some bravura back into the theatre but because it wasn't sustained by a big groundswell, I think it sometimes seems like catherine wheels that go off and then burn out.

And I think we're now in a strange state of limbo as far as acting's concerned. Most stage actors only admire film actors. They only admire Robert De Niro, Hoffman, Keanu Reeves, whatever. Now, it's no way to go forward. There's no future in that. I've seen Al Pacino on stage several times. It won't work. It doesn't work. It simply doesn't work. We've got to find some new matrix. That's why I was so thrilled when I saw the Maly Theatre because I thought: Of course, that's a wonderful artistic representation of human life. It's real, it's human but it's also **art**. Some years ago John Barton wrote a very good book called *Playing Shakespeare*, and at the end of the book he said: I think the way forward now – bearing in mind he'd come out of and indeed virtually engineered the Peter Hall revolution of making it real, vivid and rough – actually what we now need to do is rediscover the mythic factor of acting.

When I started in the theatre we all had our Artaud by our bedsides. Whether we all went the whole bloody hog I don't know but we did have our Artaud. We did believe the intensity, the overwhelming power of what he was talking about was what we should be aiming for. It all seemed to get very sort of **tame** at a certain point. The West End is very much occupied now, extraordinarily, with the kind of revivals that were the substance of the West End before the Royal Court revolution.

If you were eighteen now, would you still want to be an actor? What would you do that was different?

Everything would be different. Because the theatre is utterly and totally different. There's no rep any more, there aren't the companies that were around, joining the National Theatre Company, things one would want to do. Even the Fringe is very different. The Fringe has become rather upholstered now, where we really were doing things in back rooms and so on, and it had a rather exciting reckless quality.

I think I'd have to become an actor because it's my nature – but, I fear, an unhappy actor. I really deeply pity people who become actors now, I really do. I think the life is very unsatisfactory in every respect. For example, where would I ever get a grant to go to drama school? I remember I didn't get a grant first of all but I managed to get one because I moved an actor who was on the panel, Paul Daneman, by saying really what I wanted to do was take up Donald Wolfit's mantle. I was immersed in the **romance** of the theatre. I don't think anybody can be immersed in the romance of the theatre now.

Do people need the theatre any more – or are actors the only people who do?

I'm of the belief that essentially as long as somebody is prepared to stand up and start doing something, other people will be drawn to watch it. That's what it comes down to. But it's a curious chicken-and-egg business because I think people have learned not to need the theatre because they're very disappointed by it. So they think: It doesn't actually give me what I was looking for, so I won't go any more. In the same way, do people need religion any more? No. But that's because it doesn't give them what they are looking for.

Or they do need it but they'd be loath to admit it.

I think it's true. I think it's true of all of us. And I think it's a very interesting general trend, and nobody can figure out what we are doing wrong. Because the people who are running the theatres – especially the big theatres – in this country are not unscrupulous philistines. They're not Machiavellian in any way. They are absolutely doing their damnedest. All their choices are highly intelligent. They're really hard to fault in terms of their basic approach but I think what everybody's lost is a sense of the extraordinariness of beauty. It's product – that's the Arts Council's word – we've got to have **products** to fill our stages.

My romanticism does reveal itself in the fact that the actor I would most have liked to have seen on stage was an actor called Anew McMaster who of course nobody knows about apart from people who've read Pinter's wonderful essay about him, called *Mac*. Everything that I've ever read about this man, although he was often lazy and slapdash and the rest of it, was that he made the god descend more often than almost anybody else. The fact that he stomped around the West of Ireland for most of his career is a magnificent sort of anomaly but the truth is that somehow this man with his curious personality managed to bring his audience a sense of the splendour and drama of human life. What we actually have at the moment in a lot of our theatres is a sort of library of plays which we can sort of go and peruse. And instead of getting shafted by them, we're kind of interested by them. It's all very **interesting**.

alan mountford
Geese Theatre Company

Geese Theatre of Great Britain is a touring group working in prisons, young offender institutions and probation centres. Their work includes live performances, workshops on a variety of themes, long-term programme work, staff training and week-long residencies for forming and training inmate and ex-offender drama groups.
Alan Mountford is one of the company's most experienced members.

We're the only full-time professional company working exclusively within the criminal justice system. The company started in the States in 1980, set up by a British expat director called John Bergman. The company toured all over the States for around ten years and then an American company member came over here and set up a company in '87. So the actual history of the company goes back quite a long time. In this country it's been going for seven years now.

And how did you get involved personally?

My own personal experience was about four or five years working in various bands, trying to do music, basically. And when I was about twenty-five I thought: Fuck this for a lark – so I went to university and did a drama degree. On leaving university I was faced with the reality of life in the theatre world and the prospect of doing pretty shitty work: fairly uninspiring, dull theatre. What really interested me was things like mask and improvisation and that kind of stuff, not the mainstream stuff. So I wandered around, doing profit shares and all this, working with a theatre company in Birmingham for a while and getting very despondent.

I just reached the point where I was thinking I was going to have to rethink again as to what I was going to do – and came across the company in *The Stage*, auditioning for a job. And then after about a year in the company I decided this is where I want to be. Because it was the most logical marriage of the things that I was interested in, the theatre element which is mask and improvisation, and psychology, the therapeutic nature of theatre.

I toured for about eighteen months with the touring company and then moved over to become the programme worker for the company, which basically means that I run an alternative to custody programmes for probation services. Guys who would have been sent to prison, for instance, go and work on one of the courses that I run for six weeks and there's a whole bunch of other work they go and do. And we use things within those sessions to explore offender behaviour, to look at how they find a way of not hitting people any more. We have essentially two halves of the company, the touring company, which is all performance, and the other side of the company which I'm responsible for, or partly responsible for, which is the more long-term work.

But this long-term work still uses theatrical methods.

It's all theatre. Simply because it's the most effective way of exploring the real world. Theatre's about creating versions of reality. And the thing about using theatre as a means of exploring personal behaviour is that it's incredibly powerful. It's **incredibly** powerful. You are working through, reliving an offending experience, a situation where you were angry or violent, and you're now beginning to look at it in a different way. You start exploring all the issues that are there. How you got into that situation in the first place. What was the thinking behind that behaviour? What damage did you do to the individual victim – and all sorts of stuff tied into that.

So theatre and drama I think are very **effective** at moving people towards seeing the world in a slightly different way. And what we do in programme work is reflecting what we do in performance. It's about using theatre, it's about using shows that establish a direct link between the audience and the performers on stage. They're structured improvisations, the audience are involved in deciding what happens on stage. And they are about offender issues.

John's initial motive in going into working in prisons was political, as a Marxist. He felt that you go in there, you politicise these people and things will happen. And after about two years of trying to do that, taking in performances about American history, stuff like that, he discovered it was a load of bollocks, basically. Guys were not interested. It's a different world. Different perception of the world. Different because circumstances dictate that difference. If your experience is to be beaten up and psychologically and perhaps sexually abused for much of your early life, you have a very particular view of the rest of the world, based on that experience.

And you're less interested in politics.

Fuck politics. Give me what I want! Or: Yes, society's to blame – great, I can carry on doing what I'm doing now because it's not my responsibility. Did you see the Charles Manson thing last night? Charles Manson was very classic: he had a right to break the rules because you make the rules. Your rules are fucked and I wanna do what I wanna do, so I'm going to do what I want to do and it's going to be **your** fault because you created this world and I didn't. It's very offender thinking.

Presumably before you start going into prisons or other institutions within the criminal justice system, you have to do a lot of work, you have to know who those people are and what got them in there and what they need to get them out again.

I think a lot of theatre companies and a lot of individuals working in theatre now are looking towards working in prisons because they think: Well, here are some people who will get a lot out of what I go and do. I think that's true to a degree but when you're actually faced with a hundred **cons**, basically, and you've got to get up on stage and do something, they're not polite. They don't sit passively. They're not a middle class audience. They don't go to the Old Vic, you know. If they think it's a load of shit they'll thump you.

As prisons are essentially single-sex institutions, are there special problems—

Mm. It's not easy for women company members but we seem to employ and find very particular kinds of women, very tough women essentially, very sussed and very powerful women, who are more than capable of dealing with the kind of shit they have to deal with – with our help.

Are there particular things that you as a group and as a company can do to defuse those situations from the beginning?

To answer that question, I need to go back to the question you asked earlier on, which is that if you're going to go and do this stuff, you need to know what you're doing. But **how** do you find out about what you're doing before you go and do it? And I think this is how the company works and the touring company is where you learn.

    The first chunk of stuff you learn when you join the company is who these people are, who it is you're working with – beccause you've got to go up on stage and actually create their lives with both *The Plague Game* and *Lifting the Weight*, which are the two sister shows we do centred around two inmates.

The Plague Game is about being in prison, *Lifting the Weight* is about two guys coming out of prison. In both you have to get up on stage and show a realistic portrayal of what it is to be an offender and you're doing it in front of people who are the professionals. So you learn very quickly. As an actor what you learn to do is just to keep on asking questions and if you get it wrong, you say: OK, this is wrong, tell me how I should do it: what is he going to do? what is he going to say? how's he going to deal with this situation? what's real? And they tell you: He's going to do this – no, he's not – he's going to say . . .

The first eighteen months of my work in the company was very much about the nitty-gritty of finding out on a very direct basis who the hell we were working with. And then from there, you start looking at: OK, now I know who they are, and I'm beginning to see how they got here, what do you do about them? Which is when work really starts to take off. You start to look at: Well, OK, **what's** effective change?

John, I think, in his work, through exploring the theatre side of the touring company and also beginning to go into working with groups, began to pick up on things like cognitive and behaviour therapy as a starting place. Simply because the work that's being done within the criminal justice system on finding out what treatments work seems to show that things like psychoanalysis don't work. It's a very middle class way of dealing with people and it just doesn't seem to work with offenders.

It presupposes a certain level of articulacy for a start.

Yeah, and also the thing about guys is their primary issue in being with anybody, especially anybody who's **straight**, is finding a way of manipulating the situation. Because the world for a client or for an offender is a very dangerous place. You know, everybody's fucking over everybody else, that's a fact of life. And I've got to make sure you don't fuck me over – so I'll make sure I fuck **you** over first. It's very much about survival. And working with psychoanalysts, it was like: How do I play the game that the analyst wants me to play? How do I find a way of providing what he wants to hear so I can get out of this prison quicker?

Two guys called Yochelson and Samenow who were pioneers in using therapy with offenders started to hit very quickly early on that psychoanalysis was not working. As analysts they were being manipulated – so they started looking at alternatives. It seems that looking at the very practical here and now is what's important. So our approach is problem-solving: you're in a situation, do you want to stay? do you want to keep coming back to prison? if you do want to keep coming back to prison, OK. If you **don't** want to keep coming back to prison, how are you going to stop? It's very much about mirroring behaviour and throwing it back on the individual and saying **how** are you going to change? what do **you** need to do? And then looking at the skills that he must develop further to go and do that.

Do you sometimes get audiences who don't want to change, who do want to keep coming back to prison?

More often than not those audiences are going to be in young offenders' institutions, guys who are between seventeen and twenty-one and at a point where they are just carving out the mask that is going to be their offending mask. So the investment in the pose of offending is huge.

Once guys have been through the system and been inside for a long time, though that mask may become fairly rigid, there's also a whole bunch of other things going on behind that, which are about: What the fuck am I doing here? So the older guys will be the ones who will start thinking: Yes, I do want to change but there's no way to change. This is the way things are. Our aim is very much to start to challenge that thinking, that keeps them in this place. If there are alternatives, what are they? what do you have to do?

You came to another point – the premiss is that we're constantly learning from the people we work with, there's no psychological blueprint to go and take from the outside world and work in prison with. That's true of a lot of things quite frankly, therapeutically. You have to work with the individual. But the way theatre works and the way our performances work is by setting up recognisable stereotypes, not in a patronising way, but setting up archetypes, who count as everyman, **everycon**, you know.

It's obviously important that the audiences can put in a lot of individual characteristics, which they supply themselves, onto individual figures. They make up the story in their heads about who the people are to

them, and then they get the opportunity in some sort of dialogue with the performers to decide what's going to happen next.

Yeah, it's very much like: He wouldn't do that. Which actually means: I wouldn't do that. That character there is a reflection of me in some way. There's something about the way this guy does things that I would do – and he would do this.

From that very point, about the way in which guys project onto the characters on stage their own experience and their own stories, we moved towards devising a chunk of work called *The Violent Illusion*, which is a five-day prison installation, using two full-mask performances and a third piece which is slightly different. And the first *Violent Illusion, Violent Illusion I*, is basically about: what's the cause of the behaviour, where does it all start?

It seems fairly consistent that most guys come from fairly abusive backgrounds. So we went and looked at creating an archetypal abusive family in which a central character, which is an eighteen-month-old child, experiences all this aggression and abuse, sexual abuse and psychological abuse, and you see the process through that performance of him beginning to act out and act out and act out, until at the end of the show he's raging.

We did it in full mask for the very reason that guys could watch this show in silence and then place their own dialogue on the characters. They'd put their own words on the characters on stage and we process that stuff at the end of the show. She was this, he was that, this kid was me, this guy here . . . and they start to say the lines. We replay sections of the performance and get them to speak the lines of the character: What's he saying there?

So this is a mime?

The actual performance is in mime. It's an hour-long show, a complete performance in mime with just background music and no dialogue. And then after the show, we take sections of that play and replay it and they give us the dialogue: what did you see? what was he doing? He's thinking this, he's thinking that, he's thinking the other. He's saying this, she's saying this.

And then from that kind of overall picture we begin to link up with their own experiences. What are your experiences? Where does this connect with your experience? Who are you on stage? Which characters are you? More often than not, they're going to identify with the child, as the victim, but they'll also start to make links with some of the other characters, some of them a lot more violent characters on the stage. And then from there you can start asking about their own experience, you know: When you're being abusive, what have you got to do?

So what comes next?

The performance is first thing Monday morning. We start processing after the performance and through the first day. The second day is then about going into individual stuff: What are your offences? What happened? Day Three is another performance, which is *Violent Illusion II*, which looks at a guy coming out of prison, having made the decision to change. But having made the **decision** to change and no longer be violent or abusive is not enough. It's so much more difficult than that.

So we show him going back to a family where the rules have changed since he was last there. He's been out four years. Mum has been running the family on her own, she's got two kids there, she's been surviving the best she can – he walks into this environment now and has to deal with the changes. And has to be able to control his own anger and start to empathise and understand where his family is at.

It's about interventions, essentially. How do you stop being a destructive, selfish bastard – which so many of the guys we work with essentially are. It's a horrible thing to say but it's true. How do you start actually dealing with people **decently**? Most of the guys we work with will use some level of domestic violence, it's an accepted part of their culture: beat your girlfriend up, or at least slap her or threaten her. How does a guy stop doing that?

So *Violent Illusion II* is about presenting that dilemma, the guy endeavouring to change and through the process he begins to control more and more and more. Again it's full mask. With *Violent Illusion I* there are sections where you see the child raging, building up a rage. In *Violent Illusion II* there are sections where you see the guy getting enraged, then he's getting enraged and beginning to think: Well, maybe – and then through that process starting to intervene. And then the last time it is actually about him attempting to rationalise his own anger and saying: Wait a second. What's

really happening? What's she thinking? What's happening here? It's not just about me getting angry.

To what extent have you decided in advance what is going to happen to this guy who comes out of prison? Does it mean that you've decided already that particular situations are going to crop up and the prisoners will have to decide how he behaves?

Yes, it is like that. *Lifting the Weight* and *Plague Game* are completely improvised and we just work off whatever happens, so guys either win or lose. They succeed or they don't and the success of that show is based on what advice the audience give the characters on stage.

The guys who do *Violent Illusion* first of all are guys who've volunteered, who've decided they're going to go and do this. Secondly they must be guys who are starting a **programme**, so they come and do *Violent Illusion* for a week and that process is carried on after we leave, otherwise it would be very dangerous. So guys have already made some decision that they need to go and change. That doesn't mean that a lot of the crap still isn't there. So it has to be a little bit more directed, but that's not so much of a problem because – again, it sounds very patronising, I don't want it to sound that way – there are some archetypal ways in which offenders behave.

Everybody's situation is different but more often than not, when you start asking about the thinking behind the process, it fits within a very particular space. It's almost predictable, you know what's going to come up, invariably it's: This guy's gonna fuck me over, or: I'm not going to let people put me down, I'm not going to let my girlfriend have me under her thumb, I'm the one who's powerful . . . and all this kind of shit. So, yeah, it's much more directed also simply because in five days we're going through a very particular process which is accessing the information to begin to look at interventions, then to skills training.

After *Violent Illusion II* you're into: OK, if you **are** going to change, what are you going to do? This is the question we ask them for real. This is Day Three. What are your skills deficits? What are the things you are **no good** at? How do you negotiate instead of hitting? So we do very basic stuff, we start doing role plays using clear interventions in slowing down destructive behaviour, teach them skills and get them to practise them.

Which is what *Violent Illusion III* is about, which is essentially a theatrical test or challenge – that's more fair than 'test' because there's no win or lose in it – which the guys or five of the guys from that week go through. And it's essentially a ritual in a circular set in which everybody who's been involved in the week is there watching, or is in this space which we call the *corrida*, as a kind of a judge. Guys walk in, they make a declaration as to what it is they wish to leave behind, where they want to go, and then they're faced with a challenge. They don't know what that challenge is going to be, they just know something's going to happen, they have to practise the skills that they've learned during the week. And then we as actors go in and provide the challenges worked out in advance with the staff who are involved in the programme – and basically take them into a real world. It's like: somebody has a problem with somebody up in their face taking the piss, we go and stand up in their face and take the piss. We'll push them around the room if we need to and he has to control. And, thank God, he does, generally. It's almost psychodramatic.

The reason we went to this in the first place was there was something wrong about cognitive and behaviour therapy. It's great to go and work with thinking and behaviour but that's not necessarily going to produce results. Maybe I've got a problem with smoking. I say to myself: I want to give up smoking, **must** give up smoking, right . . . I keep smoking. **Why** do I keep smoking? Because the desire or the need to stop is not firmly planted enough in my unconscious to go and do it. I'm toying with the idea. I've got this habit, I don't know how to break it. People who stop whatever it is they're doing that's destructive invariably stop because something happened way back in here: I can't do this any more, I'm not going to do this any more. It's much more a deep-rooted response, beyond cognition. And **that** seems to be what theatre can do as a means of changing behaviour, by putting that need to change and that recognition of the ability to change further inside. Guys walk out of the *corrida* and they've just done something they've never done in their lives, and they're invariably on an incredible high and it's: I **did** it, it was very real and I stopped the process, I **dealt** with it.

We're now starting to look at what that process is about, trying to find ways of evaluating *Violent Illusion* as an intervention. But having gone back to establishments where we've been before and having met guys who've been through *Violent Illusion* already a year down the line, the effect still seems to be there. Because it hits them on three senses, on three levels: it's visual, it's audible, it's kinaesthetic. I experience the whole thing. I experience it physically as well as intellectually. It hits every part of me. And the power of the memory of that experience will be such that the determination to change becomes that much greater.

And this can only work where the audience are playing a genuinely active part. Well, there is no audience.

No, it's **me**. It's me by myself in that ring. And they're dealing with it. And it's real, it's very real, it's frighteningly real. It's the most powerful event I have ever experienced – the first time we did *Violent Illusion* it blew my socks off – I have never experienced anything like it.

So how long did it take to prepare *Violent Illusion*?

Three or four years, bit by bit, because it would be dangerous with anything to jump in and say: Let's go and do this and see what happens.

Are you aware of making mistakes, miscalculations, during performances?

Yes you are, because the issue of making mistakes and miscalculations is that you are in personal danger. When something goes wrong, somebody's got pissed off, this is somebody or a bunch of people who do not show their displeasure by saying: Excuse me. They show their displeasure by beating you to a pulp, potentially. We've done performances – not very many, thank God, because I think we're so used to working with offenders that we know how to establish rapport – but I've certainly been in situations in the past in performance when we went in to do a show in a prison – this is a few years back – where we hadn't been told that there'd been a riot in that prison a few weeks before. It was one that didn't get headline news, but it's a major nick.

These guys were very, very angry. They had no idea who we were or what we were doing there. We were dumped in the gym with about sixty of these guys and tried to do a show. The atmosphere was more than a little disturbing. It was the only time in performance I got close to being scared because we're in the gym and we've got sixty or seventy people here and we've got two officers way back there and this guy's going . . . a whole bunch of them are doing this (*stares*): These are long-termers.

So I learned very quickly how to avoid those situations and to minimise them and to come across with the truth. If they see the truth, if they see that what you're saying reflects their experience accurately, then they'll accept it. They'll say: He knows what he's talking about, they know what they're at. So much of that stuff is from experience and you can't learn any other way from getting in there and doing it – though hopefully we're now working with people in the company who are experienced enough to ensure that you don't get into that shit quite so easily as we did when we first started.

And presumably the company is organised in such a way that every time there is a new member of the company doing something they haven't done before, there are others who are experienced who are there to help out.

You're in too dangerous a world not to.

How many of you are there?

The touring company runs at five actors; two women, three men. In the company as a whole it now runs to about thirteen members, we have six programme workers – so people who basically came from the touring company, after two years or whatever are transferred into programme work, the more long-term members. And we work on our own. I work on my own – with probation staff. So there'll be a group of about eight clients and at least two probation officers.

We train probation staff, we train prison officers and just about anybody else who's involved in working with offenders. It's been very much building up techniques from experience so that now when we're training I think we're much more clear about how we go and do this properly, how you go and work with a bunch of violent offenders. And I think that's reflected in the way in which staff now view our training.

A number of the dramatic situations you present are about people being released from prison. Have you had any experience of performing to people who genuinely believe they are in prison for the rest of their lives? Do these prisoners call for a different approach?

It's different. Yeah. If I'm doing triple life what have I got to lose? I hit off inside, if I kill somebody inside, it doesn't matter: what can they do? And that's basically what starts to happen. And this is why when people are faced with that kind of sentence there has to be some kind of compensation, guys have to have something to work towards or something to have, to make life in prison bearable. Otherwise they will go off the edge.

It is difficult. In this country we don't do a huge amount of that work, we're reaching a point now where I think the opportunities to go and work with more long-term prisoners is just around the corner, it's going to happen in the next couple of years. John in the States has far more experience of that. Most of the programmes he's working in are programmes with people doing ten years minimum and those are in therapeutic units in prisons where basically you are in a programme for year after year, you're working on your thinking, working on your offending.

To measure the effect is actually very difficult. One of the things that John said, which after my experience now I'm starting to agree with, is that one of the reasons why we moved to something like *Violent Illusion* and the greater use of theatre – he started off with theatre, went into the cognitive-behavioural stuff, worked on that for a long time and has come back to the theatre as a means of change – is that guys hit a point where they know all the answers. They know all the skills, they know everything they need to know – and they're still not changing. They still go: Yes, but . . .

So that's the new area if you like – that's what *Violent Illusion*'s about, that's what a lot of development of our new work is about – trying to find out when someone has no reason to change, how do you get them to think about doing that? How are you going to affect someone like Charles Manson? Is it possible? The Mansons of this world perhaps are beyond change now, because there's no light at the end of the tunnel, he's **not** going to come out.

It's effective in that we know, having worked with these groups, that they have found our input more useful and more powerful than most other inputs that they've experienced – but as to whether that can really effect **long-term** change I don't think it's possible to say. I don't think it's possible to say in actual fact with any offender whether what we do ultimately can change an individual's life **permanently**. We don't have a magic wand and there is a question certainly with sex offenders as to whether in doing therapy with them you bring about change in behaviour or whether you make them better at what they do.

Whether you give them a greater range of dissembling?

A greater understanding as to how to go and manipulate and con those people aound you in order to go on doing what you're doing. Sex offender work is perhaps the most fascinating work we do but also the most disturbing. You don't know what effect you're having at the end of the day. Because with sex offenders there's this issue about an ingrained . . . it's about their sexuality now. Paedophiles become paedophiles invariably because they've been intensely sexually abused over a long period of time in childhood. Not all kids who've been sexually abused become abusers, but a proportion do and that's way back in development. And now, twenty, thirty and forty years on in some cases, working with guys in their fifties and sixties, you're trying to get them to change this ingrained behaviour which they've been using for years and have been abusing perhaps hundreds of children. Even people like Ray Wyre, who's been a real pioneer in working with paedophiles in this country, he'll say: I don't know whether we change them or not. That's why you end up staying doing it basically, because it becomes that fascinating. **Is** it possible?

Can you imagine working in any other kind of theatre after you've done this?

Not now, no. I've given up thinking about leaving. I can't see why I would go and do anything else. Perhaps through this conversation there's an inevitable thing about being quite negative about the behaviours that I'm working with and many of the clients that I work with – but on the other hand I actually love working with them, they're wonderful people.

Yeah, I was going to ask—

I hate what they do. I **hate** what they do.

Does spending so much time in prison depress you?

No. It's often the best place to go and do the work in the first place because they're in a contained environment. When I'm doing violent offender groups in probation, I don't know where they're going to be the rest of the time. I'm working on this guy's domestic violence and he beats his girlfriend up – tonight he's going to go back to his girlfriend, he's still in that environment, or he's going to go back to a new partner . . . In prison you can in a sense be tougher, because he's not going to go back to his girlfriend, he's going to go back to his cell. So you can do more powerful work – but then that needs to be carried on as he comes out, that needs to be carried on somewhere.

No, I like working with offenders. I like offenders. I'm very fond of offenders. I think probably because they're a group of people who in one sense you can be more honest with than anybody else. You can be straight with a guy and say that's bullshit, you know, and you can't do that in normal life – and they'll take it, once they've calmed down. You really end up empathising to a degree with the struggle of change. What I think the difference is, I can never empathise with what they do or even the whys of what they do. Because when you look at the whys of what they do, it's completely irrational.

Do you get the impression that prisons are working?

No. Prisons don't work. They do **not** work. This is a stupid, pointless exercise. They are factories for offenders. Kids go in at sixteen, seventeen and they become better at what they do. Prison turns out at the other end much more sophisticated, much nastier people. Prisons don't work.

You have to contain a proportion of these people, you have to, because if you don't contain them, they're put out on the street – hurting people. So you can't avoid this issue of containment but you have to radically rethink what that containment is about. Prisons have to become therapeutic institutions.

I'm not talking Thought Police, I'm talking of the situations where a guy goes into that environment and spends time doing therapy, working on what it is that's fucked his life up. And also doing education. It has to become a college – I don't know if you saw the news last night, a wonderful piece on Channel 4 about a college in the States with young offenders predominantly taken from the LA and San Francisco street gangs. They've got this college, and it's like being at school, they go and do education and they do therapy and they have a sixty-per-cent success rate. Sixty per cent of the guys who go through that process don't re-offend after they've completed. And a significant amount go on to university and terribly nice middle-class things like that.

But it's a sense that they actually have the chance to **address the problem** through therapy and also work towards a solution through education – that's what has to happen in prison and that's what our work's about. I see our role primarily to go and challenge offending behaviour but it's also to go and challenge the system and to say: Look, there are **other ways** of doing this and in fact these other ways are more effective. And we're not the only people doing that, there's a whole bunch of people actually.

The short, sharp shock is the most dangerous thing to go and do. They go and spend God knows how much money: thirty or forty, sixty million on building new prisons. This is madness, complete madness. Michael Howard is making policies which are purely about satisfying his electorate, it is not about what works and he **knows** what works. He knows, he's had the evidence, he's had the statistics. Interviewed on *Newsnight* after talking about building all these new prisons, the guy could not come up with any evidence to suggest that what he was doing would have **any** effect whatsoever. So we just have to keep chipping away.

Do you feel that the theatrical techniques that you've been using with the company would also be effective in other areas of society?

Yes, in a nutshell. I think they do. It's not that drama's not being used already, in therapy and also in education, you've got dramatherapy and you've got psychodrama both very powerful, both very well-established approaches. Our stuff is different – it's more sociodrama I suppose, it's much more about dealing with interactions, dealing with the here and now.

And I think this is why we're starting to do a little bit of management work. The techniques seem to be applicable anywhere. Central to our work is the mask, we use masks the whole time. And we use masks to represent the front to the outside world. If I've got a mask on my face, I can lie, cheat and bullshit, whatever. When I lift that mask, that's what's really inside me. And there are dozens and dozens of masks – it's our filter to the outside world. Some of those masks are powerful, some are destructive, some are decent, some of them are not.

Working with offenders, the wonderful power of this metaphor is that they take to it straight away, you know, as to what this front is. And using it in management structures, we go and use the same sets of masks and they go: Oh, yes, that's right – I use that one, that's one of my fronts, and they just attach their own meaning to that mask, their own interpretation. So, yes, world domination.

It would be good to do one for the Cabinet, wouldn't it?

That would be fascinating. This is the interesting thing, looking at other areas, you then start to think: What are the other masks?

We have things called fragment masks that are basically caricature masks and one has a fist coming out of its head, one's a brick wall, they're all different fronts and you begin to start thinking about: OK, what are the destructive fragment masks that people use in legitimate life, so what are the political ones? Of the ones we have already, all of them apply, but there are other ones as well and it would be fascinating to go and do that. You know, like in business, what are the masks of the business world? what are the masks that policemen have? or prison officers?

Inevitably in doing this work you cannot help but start applying it to yourself and also start applying it to everything new and seeing how it fits in with everything else. It's a life-changer. It affects you, it's affected my perception of the world. My thinking has changed quite considerably in the six years that I've been doing the work. You end up having to be much more practical or pragmatic in the way in which you approach problems.

It's opened up a whole bunch of stuff, which is probably why I continue doing it and I think why other company members stay around as long as they do. They join the company as actors – because we do look for very particular people – but sometimes people come in and it's very much, first of all about – it was for me, I think – still being an actor. And then if you get hooked there is pre-Geese and there is post-Geese and there's this thing here. It seems that for anybody who goes through Geese and leaves, this remains incredibly influential because I don't think any other experience challenges people in quite the way that Geese does. Because you have to in your work go and challenge people's perceptions so it inevitably challenges you. It challenges every element of what you do and how you think: politically, philosophically, whatever.

It strikes me that your work has a lot of elements in common with what I've read of Augusto Boal's work, and where that has a more overt political agenda, your work seems to be successful in a more sort of personally political way in terms of emotions and intellect and self-control in one's immediate situation.

I think there are parallels between Boal's work and John Bergman's work. We sometimes get referred to or are seen as being a Boal company, which is disturbing because there are fundamental differences. I think you actually very articulately stated the differences – yes, I think our stuff is much more personal. But it seems from what I'm picking up from what Boal's doing at the moment that that's the kind of direction he's beginning to move in himself. Our work will never be as influential as Boal's because I don't think we will ever be in a situation where we will address the broader spectrum – it would cease to be what we're about. So I suppose in a sense Geese and Bergman will always be a piece of kind of theatre stuff that's over on one side.

On the other hand, and given the kind of qualifications that you've made, I do feel that you have a right to feel that you have achieved something very definite in raising the possibility of theatre being able to do things it's become fashionable to think it can't do. It was very 'eighties' to go around saying: Well, theatre can't change people's lives. Seeing a particular theatrical performance is not going to make you a

better person, it's not going to do anything, it just means you've had a nice time and that's it and that's all that it's about.

That's why, with all due respect to political theatre, most political theatre is laughable. Most political theatre is performed for people who already agree with what you're doing on stage. And I think we work in an area where there is a challenge between us and the audience, that you cannot really get in any other form in quite the same way. So, yes, I believe that that's what we're doing. I believe that what we're doing is proving that theatre **can** do these things. It's a difficult process because we've been opening up a box which hasn't been properly opened before in quite this way. Lots of people have done therapy, lots of people have done therapy with offenders, no one's done quite what we're doing. So, dead exciting.

ken campbell
Quotient X

Ken Campbell's career as an actor started at Colchester Rep
in the early sixties and includes founding the Science Fiction
Theatre of Liverpool and the Ken Campbell Roadshow. He
has written and performed the *Bald Trilogy*, consisting of the
semi-autobiographical monologues *Recollections of a Furtive
Nudist*, *Pigspurt* and *Jamais Vu*, for which he won the
Evening Standard Award for Best Comedy. He has recently
unveiled three further monologues, *Mystery Bruises*,
Knocked Sideways and *Window of Opportunity*.

My mate Paul Thompson from Canada – one of about nine Paul Thompsons I know – comes over every so often and goes and sees all the shows. You can ask him if there's anything worth seeing – Not really, he said, very little Quotient X this year. I said: What's that? What does Quotient X mean? Well, he said, You don't **really** go to the theatre, do you, to see a play: Oh good, it's by Chekhov! You go in the hope that someone is exhibiting **Quotient X**, they've got a reason that they're there that isn't anything to do with fulfilling their engagement or collecting their money on a Friday, they're there actually for some **other** reason. And examples of Quotient X, here we go: Dustin Hoffman as Shylock had a fair amount of X and – ah shit, what's that bald-headed actor? American again – going back about three years . . .

Malkovitch?

Malkovitch. What's his name? John Malkovitch. John Malkovitch in *Burn This* because John Malkovitch did *Burn This* in, I call it the 'enantiodromic' approach to drama, that is that you divide the face into two. In my case, the right side is an inept housewife called Elsie, this is my right side, you see, so if I want to burble, be weak and fragile, then I perform through the right side, **or** there's a spanking squire on the left. Well, Malkovitch played that part that he was a homicidal maniac on one side and a beautiful woman on the other, you see, so he had that wig that he was like a deranged heroin addict this way round – and a beautiful lady on the other. And he was absolute to the technique. That's why he entered backwards. Because he entered shrieking abuse, showing us his abuser's thing and then he turns round and: Ah! It was all based on the enantiodromic twirl, the whole thing. Brilliant. And poor old what's his name, she's a good actress, really—

Juliet Stevenson.

But she was just acting, she was doing a normal performance, poor girl. She didn't know about Quotient X and enantiodromic procedure.

Is it possible for two people to have Quotient X at the same time, do you think?

Yeah, Laurel and Hardy. Morecambe and Wise. Morecambe and Wise was based **only** on Quotient X, I mean they're drivel, those sketches. They're about utterly fuck-all, it's just about Quotient X. If those sketches were any better, they wouldn't be as good. Brilliantly coping with crap, that was the act. They would bring people up to Quotient X standard, like Diana Rigg and what's her name – the Labour—

Glenda Jackson.

I mean terrific, they are, they become an X with the best.

I saw one repeated recently and it was the year after Angela Rippon had done it and shown everyone her legs and they did _South Pacific_ with all the male newsreaders you could think of in little sailor suits as the chorus. That was inspired.

My dad reckoned that, you see. Good acting would mean actually he couldn't watch. It would embarrass him. I think it was alright if women did it, you know, you could tolerate it, but blokes doing it was a bit of a pain. But farting about in disguises was alright, it's fine – in fact, good idea: soldiers in skirts, the Crazy Gang, something like that, was fine. Girls basically are meant to dance and men are meant to be funny: that should be ninety-five per cent of it and then there's tiny experiments in garrets, you know.

That was what was so good about Bob Hoskins, years ago – I'm not really up to the mark with his latest offerings – he could do anything and it was OK, it wouldn't upset people who good acting would normally give the pip to. He was a master of 'Uncle Fred acting', we used to call it. I think that's what Brecht was into actually – the last thing you want to see is a bloke in all his kilt and everything, you know: This is a dagger and so on. But you don't mind seeing your Uncle Fred in a tartan towel arseing around. That was fine.

What did you want this to be about? The experience of performing?

Something like that.

Well, I can't act in them, plays, any more, because I don't believe in them. I don't mind going to watch them. I don't mind directing them. But I can't **be** in them.

Why is that?

I've lost the trance that's required. I mean I can play a little part, no doubt. But to take on a role would be impossible, really.

Is it to do with the character rather than inhabiting the world of the play?

It's to do with the whole lot, it's the whole thing. I don't have any . . . I've lost attachment to it. It all looks like a set.

It happened on the last night of *The Alchemist* at Nottingham Playhouse, I was playing the Alchemist, yeah, and a little bit in, suddenly it was like: taken off the list. You can see how the set's constructed, you can see the audience, you can see what they think.

Quite frightening, I should think.

What is Nicholas le Prevost **doing**? Game's up.

I don't mind filming and I don't mind appearing, I don't mind being in front of an audience. It's not stage fright but **play** fright.

Were you already thinking of doing things like the one-man shows before that came about?

No. I didn't know whether I'd be able to do that. That came about through a girl called Gillian Brown. She came round and said: I've told them at the Offstage Downstairs that you'll do something there in a couple of weeks' time because Susannah York's let them down. I said: What are you talking about, Gillian? In two weeks' time? She said: Yes. Well, at least come and see her, see the woman. And I said: Well, I know the woman actually, she won't want me there because when she was running the New End I did a production there and didn't tell her that we were having two large pigs in it.

Anyway, we went to see her and she said: What will you do? I said: I dunno yet, I can't think of anything. The only thing I could do, I suppose, is I could do an evening of reminiscence. She said: God, that doesn't sound very good. I dunno, I said, it **might** be good. She said: We'll have to test it, you invite some of your friends, I'll invite some of my friends and we'll see what happens on the night, soon, on Wednesday. Right. But then she said: You've got to have a director and the director will have to be Gillian. Oh good God, right.

So Gillian was saying: Right, do it. And I said: No I can't do it for **you**. Anyway, it's a private thing between myself and the audience. I can't rehearse in that sense. She said: Fine. Do you know how you'll begin it? No. She said: Fine, well, just have a think till you know. She was very good actually, she directed it without knowing what it was. Will there be an interval? Yes. Do you know at what point the interval will come? No. In an hour. So then when we got to the first night – this is a genius way of directing, I thought it was brilliant – I said the last thing I want is to have notes at the end, because I'll just argue, it's pointless. Why don't we record the performance and you go back and listen to the recording and then you **compare** recordings? So she did that and it was brilliant, it was really authoritative then.

Between the evening of reminiscence and the opening night I went on Robert McKee's 'How to Write Hip Movies' course. And it was a moment in his thing where he said: A story . . . a story is more important than life itself. A story is a way bigger thing than mere reminiscence. And I thought: He's talking to **me**. So instead of an evening of mere reminiscence I decided to attempt A Story in McKee Terms. And I took about a hundred pages of notes on his course. So this became *Recollections of a Furtive Nudist*. I had a card that represented every lump of the show so I could lay it out in front of me, could open my notes at random, my McKee notes, and say: Oh, yes, well, I haven't got any of that in, let's try that. So I re-sorted it out again and again and again according to what I supposed McKee had been about. He's become a great fan – he's come to see them all and *Pigspurt*, he said, is **sensationally** constructed, that is **divine** construction. I said that that's the one that I used your technique the least. He said: I like it! Excellent.

You know there's a guy does my *Furtive Nudist* in Munich? He's terrific at it.

Rufus Beck, isn't it?

He still does it about once a month. It's the longest-running production in the Munich repertoire. We didn't translate it, we **transliterated** it. So it wasn't about me, it was about Rufus.

Is it very odd watching somebody playing a part that was originally you?

I nicked loads. I had to write and ask them for the German version. Because I came home and I was doing it and I thought: Actually, fucking Rufus has a much better bit here! I'll have to translate it.

A marvellous thing happened, you see. I used to say, because this was true: When this guy Andy Jones got teleported out of a King's Cross toilet in fact I was writing a play called *The Great Caper* at the time. Well, I can't say I was writing a play, says Rufus, because everyone knows I don't write plays. So I said yeah, but maybe you write **poems**, that you never read to anyone, but you do write poems. OK, I'll say poems. And then the next day he says: This poem that I've written – what's it actually about? And we'd been talking and they were amazed that I'd never heard of the author Karl May, who was the most famous German author of all. He wrote cowboy books and Red Indian books, *Winnitou* and whatnot.

And I went to go and buy one and I went to a bookshop and they said, no-no-no, you have to go to the supermarket. So I turned up at the book section and asked for the Karl May bit and the bloke pointed and I couldn't see any. The reason I couldn't see any was because there were **so many**: there were about half a million Karl May books. Fuckin' hell! So I bought that and he said: What's this poem about? And I says: It's about urban Red Indians, it's about a bunch who are so into the works of Karl May that they can't get jobs or anything, they just think they're Red Indians and get pissed.

It's like an epic poem? says Rufus. Yeah. So how does it go, this poem? So I went away and wrote the poem in English and then they translated it into German and Rufus said: Oh, we'll have to have this **in**, I have to perform this Red Indian poem. And so when I got back home and I was talking about my play for a couple of nights, I thought: Fuck it, it's much better to have

Timothy Walker, Lyric Theatre, Hammersmith

Hugh Quarshie, Tricycle Theatre

Sylvestra le Touzel, Old Vic

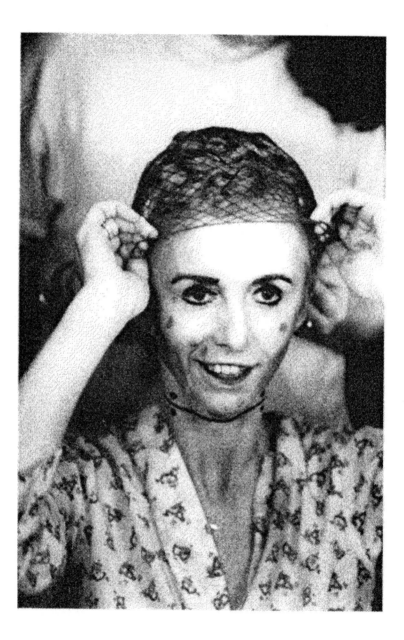

Jane Asher, Vaudeville Theatre

Antony Sher, Albery Theatre

Michael Hordern, Theatre Royal, Haymarket

Sara Kestelman, Old Vic

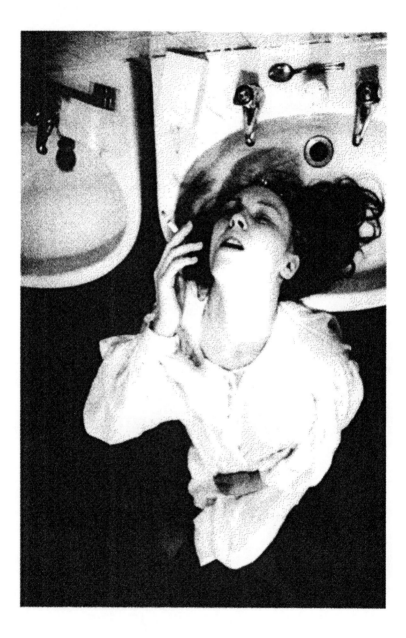

Rudi Davies, Comedy Theatre

written a poem. And so then I had to get the German, because I'd lost my English thing, and translated it back into English:

> In the tavern by the tramstop
> Heroes on the dark firewater [That's Guinness, you see]
> One pint, two, then three and four.
> See the moon, says Appanatshka,
> Moon is twice as big as usual,
> Sign that something big will happen.
> Night of nights this moon portends.
> In that instant comes the lady,
> Lady with the long black hair.
> May I sit here? says the lady.
> Sits down on adjoining chair.
> Heroes speechless, staring in wonder,
> Stare at lady's long black hair.
> *Das ist Nscho-Tchi, Appanatshka,*
> *Das ist Nscho-Tchi, ist ganz klar.*

In my version, one of them's probably a one-time prisoner of war who didn't go back to Germany in time for the repatriation, so he lapses into odd German phrases in the poem.

It's interesting because playwrights worry a lot about construction and how scenes follow on from each other.

They do, do they?

Some of them do.

Which ones do?

The ones who have too much exposure to dramaturgs like me – who take it all terribly seriously. Yet the actual business of performing a show when you're devising it always seems much more relaxed. Do you think you'd have been able to trust yourself to do those sort of performances if you hadn't written plays beforehand?

Don't know. I honestly don't know. Some people call them plays – to me they're not plays. What they are . . . Well, how it began was there were two ways. One was pitching a movie. In my case instead of taking the ten minutes that you're meant to, it takes slightly longer than the film would. Quite a lot longer. But also it was Spalding Gray gave me a whole notion. That's why I was going to sit at a table. But I found I couldn't sit at a table like he can. It's really quite extraordinary to sit at a table for a couple of hours. I think it's terrific, that *Swimming to Cambodia* film, which is about how he got this small part in *The Killing Fields*. Now *Killing Fields* is a pretty good movie and I've seen it twice but hearing his account of how he got a small part in the movie is a way superior work of art and I'd happily watch it twenty times. You go off on your own tangents during a thing like that, quite happily. Have you seen Eddie Izzard doing his one-man show?

Is it good?

Oh yeah! And what's good about it is – you know he's dyslexic, considerably dyslexic – well, he's dyslexic in speech, so unlike . . . I suppose the nearest thing might be Frankie Howerd actually. The odd thing is he communicates the humour of what he's talking about but without structured sentences and without punch. And as a result of it, you fall in love with him, all sexes fall in love with him. And you don't often fall in love these days, you don't fall in love with stand-up comedians because they're such flash buggers.

I don't like to talk about it too much, the experience of performing, because it's a bit like speaking about the dead, but sometimes now I get the feeling when I'm doing it: This is quite **weird** actually, doing this. That's a bit new to doing it. I just used to do it, not think about it. And this is fucking weird actually. Let's talk some more about Quotient X. I never saw it but I guess Anthony Hopkins had it when he was in *Pravda*.

Oh yes. He was very **good.**

But **X** wasn't it? He wasn't in a play, it was something else.

It was obviously very technical, it was done in this huge space and he'd

got the way that the guy walked and stood and the way the words came out of his mouth and the South African accent, and it was one of those things – it was a very Brechtian thing in a way – you knew it wasn't actually him and that it was an act but it was very exciting and you really just wanted to see what he was going to do next – he made the play.

There was some X going on in *Glengarry Glen Ross* when I saw it at the Donmar, I thought. Bits of that have lived in the head – there was something about Ron Cook, his look: he has a blue suit on, right. I couldn't tell you any line out of that piece now, but if I think of Ron Cook standing in a certain part of the stage: Wow! And if I think of those two on that tiny revolve: man, this was something – what were they talking about? who were they? Man, they were good. Now that had great staging . . .

Well, that's enough of that. I think I'll bugger off now.

patsy rodenburg
Harder work than ever before

Patsy Rodenburg is Head of Voice at the Royal National Theatre and the Guildhall School of Music and Drama. She is the author of *The Right to Speak* and *The Need for Words*.

No one is able to create theatre without actors and performers. Yet while a number of interesting ideas are being thrown up into the air and interesting contributions are being made, it's not always the actors who are the centre of that movement.

No. Most actors definitely feel that they're losing power all the time. In very technical theatre they're going back to just being moved around in space and not allowed to be creative any more. A lot of my work is about making actors rediscover their power.

In relation to the text?

And their voice. This is very pragmatic, but if you're on a set and you're worried about the rake, it's very hard to breathe, it's very hard to release anything. And actors are not even **asked** whether they want to do this. They're put into the middle of it and then expected to act.

In a lot of western theatre we now spend hours sitting around a table **talking** about a text. But a great actor needs to be **doing** it. They should be acting. A lot of actors complain a great deal that they're so cut off from the audience at the moment, they don't get a chance to explore their craft in the way that they might have done twenty years ago.

Is this something you're talking about within a production process or are you talking about the fact that work is less continuous than it was before?

It's both. I know that if an actor today gets a good training, if they're lucky they'll leave college and they might speak two lines once a week at the RSC for eighteen months. This is not helping the actor **grow**. Weekly rep might have been ghastly on some levels but my goodness it prepared actors for their craft. And they don't have that. So when older actors criticise them I always defend young actors.

Good actors are always working on themselves. Physically as well as vocally. But some actors feel so lost at the moment that they start to ask themselves: Is it worth working?

A frightening thought.

I come across it all the time. The good ones probably don't have that attitude, but it's common.

They've completely lost their power if they have no opportunity to work.

Yes and then in the working situation the concept, the design has actually stopped any creative purpose. The director might say to them: You can do this this this and this – and then about three days before the technical turns round and says: You won't be able to do that because the revolve will be coming round then. And suddenly it dawns in the actor's mind that their whole process has been set from the word go and they just have to fill very narrow limits. And it's frightening for actors, this sort of theatre. How can you be creative? With my students when they go and see previews, I always say to them: Listen, don't you get snotty – if you're standing on stage wondering when that piece of scenery's coming, how can you be free?

And is this a direct result of a fashion for more spectacular technical productions?

Yes. It seems that a lot of people go now to the theatre **not** to concentrate and work. I mean, when you have the work that goes on in say a Complicité piece, you have to have an audience that wants to sit in the theatre and go through something intellectually and emotionally. Now a lot of the design aspects of theatre make people feel that they're at a spectacle, they can sit back and not do anything. If we're talking about great acting, great actors also need audiences that are ready to respond and appreciate what they are doing. I think it's a very sad thing in theatre when sets get a round of applause. A very committed actor has to convince the audience that they should be listening, that they should be **connected**. A lot of audiences now don't go to do that.

Now we've lost all our TIE companies. In the next few years, there will be no more kids coming to our theatres as a result of seeing theatre in schools. It's an explosive thing that's happened. We **had** some of the best companies in the world. And that was a fantastic training ground for young actors, about audiences, having members of the audience shout out to them. A couple of weeks ago at the National somebody shouted out: 'Can't hear you!' I think that's quite healthy. It used to happen much more – the audiences are becoming so passive now.

It's stupid but I think theatre lost something with the introduction of cue lights. If you're just waiting for a green light to go on and you go on and you play your scene, you're completely disconnected.

That's horrible. Is that what they have?

Oh yes, they stand waiting for their light to go on. I'm not blaming actors because the sets are so bulky and the stages are so big that they maybe can't hear what's going on on stage except over the tannoy. But if you think about the shows that you've seen that are very exciting, often the actors are all in the room, listening, and they're holding the story. You can't really be responsible for telling a story if you're just waiting for a green light to go on. Telling a story is the most basic thing in theatre – and that's lost. And when we see actors in small companies – Cheek By Jowl, Shared Experience – you always get the story, because the actors are responsible in the space. That's the power of the actor.

It was very interesting when we all went down to look at the Rose Theatre, to realise that the first members of the audience's hands were almost on the stage. Their little heads would be looking up at the actors like a child at the feet of its parent, being told a story. When you're that close to an actor, an actor **can't** bluff, they can't deny an experience because it's like sitting in a room with someone, they're right there. And now, with lighting design, many actors can't see the audience.

And the audience can't see the actors' faces.

That is a huge problem vocally. If you can't see a face, it's very hard to hear. And these things really do depress performers. You should hear actors off stage, you know, during the technical: But I can't be seen, I **can't be seen**. And it's **not** their vanity, they know something important is going to be lost. But very few of them ever speak up, that's the sad thing. Some do, but very few will say: I can't work in this costume, I can't breathe in this costume. **I've** had to say to designers: You've got to take that costume off, you've got to loosen it, this person can't begin to sing wearing that.

These are very small things. But if you're going **out there** – actors are gladiators, aren't they? They're modern-day gladiators – they're not getting killed, but they are going out there and the good ones risk **everything**, they risk all their passion and feeling in showing it to an audience. And if you can't breathe because you've been put into a corset, that is a problem.

You don't only work with actors' voices. Do you think of the work you do in terms of giving people an acting skill or giving actors a people skill?

It's both. If you work on anybody's voice, hopefully you're going to make them feel better, you're going to make them feel more centred, more able to speak, whatever the circumstances. I just like working with actors a great deal more because all the problems are going to be exposed. An actor going on stage is undergoing an enormous amount of stress and so to learn how to release tension – which is fundamental to my work – and how to breathe is going to help them just get out there and take the space and speak.

Is it easier to teach actors than non-actors?

Well, I love teaching actors because they know that they need the work, they know that it's dodgy out there – but they're also risky, they're courageous people, really. They want to go out and do something, and they're all very scared about doing it. But they do it. And they have a certain need of doing it. I love them, because they take those risks.

Did you at any stage want to be a performer yourself?

I did a bit. I didn't enjoy it. I enjoyed teaching. That is a form of performance, of course.

This whole area of jobs or areas of human activity where people use acting skills but aren't actors is something I find very interesting. I know, for example, that you've also given lessons to politicians. Do you feel that these people are acting as well?

Ye-es. This is a dodgy one, isn't it?

For one thing, an actor always has a text that they're working on, so when you're working with an actor if you come to some terribly revealing emotional thing – I never improvise, I'm much too much of a coward in my work – you can always blame the text. You don't have to look at yourself. When you uncover something in someone's own text, it's much more revealing. When you work a lot with politicians or executives – and I don't do a huge amount, because it doesn't interest me in the same way that it interests me working with teachers or in prisons or whatever – if you do that sort of work with them, they'll be exposed. Because what they're trying to do is **hone lying**. Now I actually think when a great actor actually gets hold of a text and really knows that text, they **can't** lie, they're telling the truth. And that's a very different thing.

And the fact that the text has an origin which is clearly separate from them is something which gives that performance an incredible power and emotional resonance for a brief period – you know it will go away again.

Right. You can finish the play and drop it. And that's another reason for good technique – you've got to be able to do that every night, consistently, but not go mad, playing a great, great part.

When working on other, normal voice users, I never go that deep in the same way – I haven't got the safety of the text. When I work with normal people, all they want is release and improved voice production. An actor wants that as the first stage. In training an actor you worry about that in the first year and then you go into the much deeper places.

One of the phenomena which really interest me is Ronald Reagan – and basically just how he got away with it.

Well, yes. Hitler as well was a real bad actor. He was taught by an old rep actor. What you can see, that Ronald Reagan used and other politicians use, is that certain things will always work because there is an organic thing that is touching people. The iambic works because it's the heartbeat. And some people are good enough speakers just to find them out. If you aren't, you can learn them. Hitler used the old techniques – evangelical preachers use them – that without the audience knowing it you continually just lift your voice a bit, you know, and then you just lift your voice a bit more, you go on for a bit like that and then you just lift a bit more and you get people right up there, so everything's at a very high pitch – and you get them hysterical.

If you listen to an evangelical preacher and analyse and transcribe what they say, there is nothing being said. But they get an emotional impact because of using vocal techniques: rhythm, timing, breath techniques. If you watch – and I've been to analyse these preachers – the whole congregation is breathing together. I'm sure the whole of Nuremburg was breathing together after Hitler got them going, they were just like a giant pair of lungs.

And that's why there are bits where they all have to join in.

Yes. And they couldn't stop themselves. To walk away would be breaking a whole rhythm.

But I think that's what Ronald did. He managed just to put over some stuff on camera and say nothing. And the sad thing is that the media at the moment are encouraging that. Politicians will say to me: Well I've got two and a half minutes and basically I have to sound intelligent but not say anything.

Now the speakers that are still very good are the ones who came from the tradition of being heckled and having to speak for two hours or more – and then my goodness you've got to say something. And that's coming back to heckling in the theatre. It makes the actor alive, doesn't it? I mean, it's like directors who will play tricks on their actors to keep them alive: they'll suddenly change the prop or give a note to another actor secretly to keep the actor on their toes.

Really great acting, for me, is when the actor is alive and dangerous, in a state of **readiness**. And from my point of view, technically, you can only get that when you're alive in your body and your breath and your voice – and you're filled. A great deal of my work is getting people to that state. That you don't come on and be cool. I'm just shouting at these students, there's **nothing** cool in Shakespeare! So don't shuffle on – they're states of emergency, states of being alive! It's heightened. I've never had a playwright say to me: Make my actors more naturalistic, more soggy. The note I get from writers all the time is: My plays are heightened! It's important.

Coming back to Ronald, he had that technique and he didn't say a thing. And generations of movie-goers in America were duped. One of my great beliefs, this is one of my great passions, is that if everyone was given voice work and we all understood all the techniques, they **couldn't** dupe us. If every schoolchild was taught how to speak and how to use the voice and when it's open and telling the truth, they would say: Actually, **no**, that's crap. People who come from a tradition as I said of halls and heckling, they weren't going to be taken in by Ronald. I would suggest in front of a live audience on stage he . . .

Would not be very good.

It's true. Because he knew all the cosmetic things that would work superficially in front of a camera. Which is back to our basic thing of a live performance is going to hit you and move you much more than anything else. Change you. Great theatre should change us.

Do you feel that more is required of actors now than previously?

Yes, they've got a much harder life. Also in the skills required. Actors now have to do all sorts of things that they've never had to do before. They have to learn to sing, they have to be able to dance to a certain extent – which is good. But it means that the training period of three years really isn't long enough. And we can't get the money for longer training, we're all tied to that.

They're expected to be able to fill the Olivier stage one day and then go on camera the next. One of the advantages of British theatre, unlike American theatre, is that the actors do flow between television, film, theatre and radio.

We have to fight for the great tradition of radio in this country because it's where many young actors get their first job in speaking the classics. My great belief is you can't act these great plays until you speak them out loud on a regular basis.

It's how audiences encounter plays for the first time, as children, at home on the radio.

And they're teaching people to listen. Everything else in society is conspiring against the actor, against oracy and skills of speaking.

I think the greatest single problem that actors have now which they didn't have before is that society's and our notions of authenticity have developed and become more sophisticated as a result of exposure to the increasing proliferation of reproduced images which are much more convincingly lifelike than was previously the case.

That's us not fully understanding truth in a heightened situation. We're becoming so decadent that to play Hecuba and release on that level is alien to us. My battle often with young actors is that truth can be big and in heightened moments it's very big and it's very clear. They always want to reduce it and minimise it. If you watch those women in Bosnia talking, it's so clear, it's so direct, it's so heightened: They took my husband, they shot him under that tree. And most actors would want to cloud that for a very cheap effect.

I was talking to a television person in America about the fact that if you ask somebody a very clear question if they've just had an accident, they're very clear, they don't burst into tears, they start talking cleanly. But American television doesn't think that's dramatic enough, so what they do if they're going to interview someone is they get them crying and weeping before the camera goes on. Which is not the truth.

There's a technique, which has been banned in this country, to question somebody and make them break down. And then you put the camera on, so you're showing the audience – you're showing all of America – not the truth, but one step outside of it. I know the technique. It can be useful. Social workers use it to get breaks. Basically I ask you question after question after question and you feel safe. Did you take your child to school today? Yes, I did. Did she have a packed lunch? Yes, she did actually. And then what happened? Well, this happened and this happened. And at the moment when I think you trust me – you might still be very distressed, you've just seen your child killed, but you're talking about it – I just shut up and I don't give you the support system. And it's guaranteed that within about thirty seconds you'll start crying.

In close-up.

And then the camera is switched on. So truth, yes. We've been fiddling around with truth, maybe out of decadence. In my work I definitely deal with the habits of decadence: people who are not in their bodies. If you were a farmer, or a fisherman pulling in a net, you could not **not** be in your body. If you rode a horse eight hours a day, you could not **not** be centred – you'd have to breathe right down there.

A lot of young actors walk into these great texts with their twentieth-century speech habits about non-communication – but you can't apply those habits to a text which is about communication, about people who are much more in their bodies, breathing a lot more, speaking on a regular basis. They need passion, to be passionate. You can't play these great plays, you can't play Shakespeare or Shaw, without a passion about thinking and feeling. So they have a huge journey to make.

simon annand
Faces in the dressing room mirror

Simon Annand has worked as a photographer for theatre,
opera and film since 1987. The companies he has worked for
include the Old Vic, the Royal National Theatre, the
Comédie Française, LIFT, Opera North, Luzern Opera House,
the International Workshop Festival, the Gate Theatre,
Cheek by Jowl, Cambridge Theatre Company, English
Touring Opera and ATC.

'When I was twelve, I was allowed to accompany a musician who was playing the celeste backstage in Strindberg's *A Dream Play*. It was a searing experience. Night after night, hidden in the proscenium tower, I witnessed the magic of acting. The Officer was backstage waiting for his entrance, leaning forward looking at his shoes, his hands behind his back. He cleared his throat soundlessly, a perfectly ordinary person. Then he opened the door and stepped into the limelight. He was changed, transformed: he *was* the Officer.'

Ingmar Bergman
The Magic Lantern

simon russell beale
The whoppers

Simon Russell Beale trained at the Guildhall School of Music and Drama. He joined the Royal Shakespeare Company in 1987 and is now one of the company's associate actors. This interview was conducted in a dressing room at the Barbican, where he was on stage every night, playing either Edgar in *King Lear*, Oswald in *Ghosts* or Ariel in *The Tempest*. In 1995 he left the company to play Hamlet.

Maybe a good place to start is with the joys of acting. What's good about it?

It often doesn't feel very joyful, I can tell you. You feel tempted – I don't know why – to say: yes, it's always a delight – and it patently, obviously isn't. It can be a great bore. But by the end of each performance – and I have to say by the end of **every single** performance – it's the best feeling you can have during the day – the vodka and tonic afterwards perhaps excepted.

I was thinking about that last night in *Lear*, which is a real struggle. There's a monstrously large piece and it's dealing with monstrously large things and playing Edgar is a monstrously incomprehensible demand on anybody. And I didn't really want to do it last night but by the end, and I don't really know quite why, you lock yourself back in. It's very odd because everyone thinks the big shows here, all the big display pieces like *King Lear* or *The Tempest*, are about going out **to** the audience. Funnily enough, I find that I've been locking **in**, back in to my relationship with my father, Gloucester, and coming off the stage having actually quite genuinely been there. That is terribly satisfying because it's like sleepwalking: one minute I'm standing there and now I'm in the wings. The two are completely separate. That doesn't always happen but last night it did. Edgar was a completely separate person from me. And that is terribly satisfying.

The other very simple answer to the joy of it is . . . doing *The Seagull* two years ago and Chekhov writes his two-minute silence before Konstantin commits suicide, which is pacing about, and he breaks his pencil, all that sort of thing – or doesn't break his pencil – and then goes off and shoots himself. For about a minute of that time – and we were very strict, it had to be two minutes – I stood on stage absolutely still and: **power**! That's what it was, power. Standing dead still on a huge stage doing absolutely nothing except **thinking**. And there was absolute silence, because we'd all worked to that, the whole company had worked to that particular point. It's the climax of the play. Unbelievable!

And another thing is comedy, making people laugh. I haven't done that now for two years. I had one joke in *Ghosts*.

I laughed in *Ghosts*!

Probably not at me, though. There are quite a lot of jokes in *Ghosts* but they're usually to do with the Pastor and Mrs Alving, not with miserable old Oswald. So making people laugh – I suppose that's a basic adolescent urge of acting, it's where a lot of actors come from. But **power** – it was the power. The power I felt as Konstantin was of a different order. The sound of silence, two thousand people silent, absolutely silent – amazing! (*Laughs.*) Sounds like a Nuremburg rally, doesn't it? – as morally suspect as that!

But it's different when you're a person who's about to walk off stage and shoot yourself from being someone who's telling the two thousand people to go and—

Kill another race, yes. Absolutely, obviously. But I'm always suspicious of my own response to that, a little, just a tiny little bit. You have to keep monitoring yourself. That's why actors become such monsters, I suppose. We're all in danger of becoming monsters, because there is power. We always used to play that game. 'What do you want out of life – love, money or power?' A lot of actors, if they were being truthful, would say power.

It's interesting because I think as well at some level all plays which are about the theatre are about power.

Yes, well, *The Tempest* is about theatrical magic and colonisation at the same time, and they're possibly the same thing. It's funny because the paradox is of course that you make a sort of bargain, isn't it? You say for a certain period of your life you're absolutely . – I think I'm particularly subservient to directors, I'm particularly passive in developing something until the last moments – you say you'll spend, in the case of the RSC, eight weeks of a rehearsal process being totally subservient and then: It ain't anything to do with you any more! It's all mine.

And of course it's a fake power because you're not **you**, are you? I suppose why I'm mentioning Konstantin first is because that's the one single thing that I've done where I've felt this has absolutely been about as close to me as anything I've ever done, so I suppose that's why I felt a particularly acute sense of power. But the same silence you achieve as Oswald or Edgar or Ariel or Richard III is actually fake. I'm playing an extremely arrogant Ariel and when something goes wrong, I just walk off stage.

I know. I saw you.

Oh, you saw that one, did you? This is **why** the power is fake. You play an insufferably arrogant version of Ariel in which everything he does is absolutely perfect – and in fact you're entirely dependent on everybody else. When **you're** pretending not to be. If something goes wrong, my argument falls to bits. The only way out of that is to walk off stage and say: Nothing to do with me, mate. The embarrassment level is very high. And this is actually true of almost every actor I know.

But it never really throws me when I'm watching and that happens, it simply introduces another element into the experience.

I know that. I just got a letter. I don't know why we're talking about mistakes in the theatre but I suppose they are important. It was again *The Seagull* and I wasn't wearing any knickers. And my trousers . . . well, they actually **exploded**. A hole in the back of my trousers split and it was the last act and it was extremely serious and the only way I could get off stage was to shoot myself – and I had to stand there with my bottom showing to a three-sided audience. Now I got a letter two years later, at Stratford last year, which simply says: 'Dear Mr Russell Beale, we saw the performance of *The Seagull* in which your trousers exploded.' They said nothing about the performance. It was just to let me know. Obviously this has stuck in their minds. This is years later. I know people enjoy it, people are intrigued by it, when things are less than perfect.

I also know that when I'm in the audience it doesn't worry me. I remember seeing a performance of *The Miser* a couple of years ago. It was one of those nights when the set was going wrong and everyone was falling over, tripping over their dresses and things . . . and I remember thinking they must be going through hell and actually it doesn't worry me at all.

But there's that famous line that Nina says, and I know what she means, when Nina says to Konstantin right at the end: 'You don't know what it's like when you know you're acting badly.' And I suppose that's the threshold of embarrassment. You **don't** know what it's like. It's **horrible** when things are going wrong.

I think though, the fragility of an illusion is something that it's always very enlightening for an audience to see when it's made manifest. Which I think is why there are so many plays with plays in them and with scenes backstage and illusions created.

I know what you mean, but in my heart I want it to be absolutely perfect. And it also depends on the stakes. Because if you're playing Restoration comedy and it goes wrong or if you're doing *Venetian Twins* by Goldoni, the stakes aren't that high – I don't mean the emotional stakes but the stakes with which you're saying: This is a complete world. If you're doing *Ghosts* which is like hermetically sealed, that's a high risk thing to break. And if you're doing *The Tempest* where you're saying this has to be absolutely perfect, this is visually and in every way perfect and rather cold and remote as a show – if you decide that that is what you're going to present to the audience, then breaking that is more than irritating, it's actually **upsetting**.

Ariel is actually a rather thrilling experience for me because I've never had to do a part where every single move is choreographed. It's ninety-nine per cent conscious. That's why it's quite simple actually because it's more like being a dancer. I'm not a dancer, but dancers presumably have to do it all the time, be conscious of every single tweak that they do. I'm not skilled enough at that to do anything more complicated than the Ariel that I'm doing which is very simple. But I do know every single finger waggle or eyebrow, everything, every movement of the eyes, which is very odd. It's like being a computer. And it's a completely different experience.

More technical and mechanical?

Oh, much. And it's **liberating**. Because it's like doing some sort of therapeutic treatment.

Because there's much less psychology involved?

There's just one basic psychological thread, which you cling on to, which is about anger. And you just pull yourself through the play on that one thread while doing absolutely what one hopes is perfectly controlled physical and vocal life. So therefore if you ask me: What do you do on that particular line in that particular scene? I can tell you now. Oswald, God knows: sprawling all over the sofa, I don't know where **he** is. Although I know – because I was directed very accurately – I know what I'm thinking.

Another funny thing about Ariel was it was the most nerve-racking first performance I've ever had to do of anything including *Richard III* and I suspect including *Hamlet* next year. In that type of performance there's no release at all. Physically or mentally. And I'm sure every actor needs that, that release.

For somebody like me and I suspect any 'classical' actor coming to Ariel, the premiss that he doesn't have any feelings is a bit hard to play. It's an absolute negation of everything you've ever thought your craft is. In fact he does have a range of feelings but as a first premiss that's an odd thing to act.

I think, though, it's very interesting to look at Shakespeare in those terms. A lot of us have grown up with the theory that the theatre has to be recognisably about problems which the audience can identify in their own lives. And therefore we write plays about people like us. Yet Shakespeare isn't like that, is it? It's full of Caliban, Ariel, Prospero . . .

Yes, the jump in order to understand Caliban has to be made, you can't make Caliban come to you. You can't say: Oh, I know somebody like that next door, he plays his music very loud and . . . It doesn't have any poetic weight. I don't think we're in the business to remind people of their own lives, actually.

I think in a way not understanding Caliban is just as interesting, possibly more interesting, than understanding exactly who he is.

Absolutely. And the same applies to Richard, all of Shakespeare's major roles – I don't want anybody to actually think that they know who Richard was.

Is this what allows the plays to keep on being done with such regularity?

They're so broad-based, aren't they? And the thrill is surely to watch a particular personality confront this thing and to see how that particular personality mixes with that thing to produce something that's unique. And Shakespeare does have enormous capacity for accepting the personalities of the actors that are performing him into him. I know very safely that every time I do a Shakespeare character of any depth it's going to be like nobody else's. Every actor must know that.

But I **can** understand why Billington keeps on saying there should be a ban on Chekhov. They are the most perfect, pearl-like structures but they are less adaptable than Shakespeare. If you say: Does an audience come and see a play in order to link their own lives with the lives of people that they see on stage? then that's much more acute in Chekhov than it is in either Shakespeare or Ibsen. My experience of Chekhov is very limited but I do know that part of the reason why you have two minutes of unbelievably exciting power at the end of *The Seagull* as Konstantin is because most people have problems with their parents at some level or other.

So does Hamlet.

Yes, of course he does, but again his expression of it is so broad-based. If Konstantin says to Nina: 'It's not within my power to stop loving you', we've all been there and in an odd way we haven't been there. It's partly to do with articulacy. I remember Nick Dear talking about *The Art of Success*. He said: 'All my characters in this play are equally articulate.' And of course that's absolutely true of Shakespeare – though that isn't true of Chekhov and it isn't true of Ibsen and of many other later dramatists who make some characters less articulate than others. And that means that the whole idea of the articulation of thought becomes less important than the articulation of an emotional state. So therefore the response from the audience is much more to do with their reciprocal emotions. I don't know about you, but I'm very rarely moved **as a whole** by a Shakespeare play. When I do go to Chekhov, I do sob – because it's all so . . . you know. Whereas with Shakespeare I get like that description of Kean: Shakespeare by flashes of lightning. You hear a line and you think: Oh wow! How did he think of that?

Years ago, seeing Deborah Warner's *King John*, which I didn't know at all, I can remember two lines absolutely clearly. When King John wants to be crowned again, the courtier says: 'Why add another colour to the rainbow?' And then there's a line when John's dying and he's taken into the garden and he says: 'Ah, now my soul has elbow-room.' The response to that is completely different to the response to 'It's not within my power to stop loving you, Nina.' Equally exciting but completely different. This is a thing that I've always been very keen on, that intellectual excitement can be as viscerally moving as emotional excitement. The sheer thrill of thinking: Ah, he's thought of that!

What do you see as the actor's role in the process of creating the show? Or what it should be?

It's different for everybody. I'm very passive for a long period. All my best ideas have been other people's, usually the director's, for which I've got the credit very often. I feel most comfortable being a sort of logical brake on somebody else's ideas. I'm quite good at spotting mistakes. If then they give me an idea, I think I'm also quite good at accurately – and this is actually a bad thing – **accurately** performing somebody's notes. I can remember Terry Hands saying to me: Directors don't want that, they don't want you to repeat what they've just said, they want you to go six steps further. That's what's exciting for a director. And I'm beginning to learn that. You are not responsible to the people who are directing you, you have an independent mind – and that's quite a tough thing to learn, actually, especially if you're a young actor.

You don't see the actors as these wonderful naive spirits who are then sold into slavery to capricious directors?

(*Laughs.*) No. I do think actors become actors partly because they can abdicate responsibility for quite a lot of their lives. I have no responsibilities at all in my life. The buck doesn't finally stop ever with me, even if I'm doing *Richard III.* I'm sure a lot of actors, deep down in their souls, are probably quite pleased about that. A lot of them obviously aren't – they're the ones who become directors of course. We're not naive little creatures being abused by tyrannical martinets, no, not at all.

Do you think that the job that you do is an important one?

Yes. Absolutely. Yes. Incredibly important. For what we've talked about earlier which is that you force people to make imaginative leaps, which is therapeutic, both for themselves and indeed you. Because, God knows, a lot of acting is like therapy. Oswald's like a very, very expensive session with an extremely good psychotherapist – as indeed Konstantin was. So, yes. And I don't mean to move people or to make them laugh, although that's important as well, to just join them on this jump, to **think** about a Caliban – that's wonderful isn't it?

You are really quite unusual in that you are the embodiment of what a company like the RSC is supposed to do: you joined quite soon out of drama school, started off playing smaller parts and gradually built up to—

The whoppers.

Become a protagonist. Clearly if you hadn't been enjoying this you wouldn't have done it. But what are the special advantages?

Why did I stay? There was a time twenty years ago when people like Roger Rees, Ben Kingsley, Tony Church stayed for ages. Eight years is relatively little. But it's funny that the question is being asked now. People say: After two years you **must** get out. And actually no, I mustn't get out. This has now become my professional home and will, I hope, remain so. There are precious few opportunities to do the type of work that I do, elsewhere. We just don't have theatres in this country that can afford to do these massive plays.

And I keep on wondering, you know, it's a whole life we're talking about here, I've got time. Hopefully, if I live to sixty, eight years in my twenties spent at the RSC doing these sort of parts won't seem that long.

Is there something about being able to play several classical roles at the same time over an extended period and being able to juggle one against the others that's particularly fascinating?

It's virtuosing. There's a sense in which you walk into the stage door going: Huh, what am I playing tonight? Which is tickling.

Maybe having different dressing rooms is quite good.

Yes. To remind you.

You don't have all the costumes in the same place.

It's also got something to do with the fact that with a company like this, working over very long periods of time, you have to take risky casting choices. I have been such a beneficiary of that. Parts which I thought I would be able to do falling off a log I've fallen flat on my face, parts which I never thought I would do seem to have worked, like Ariel, which, God knows, is a ridiculous piece of casting. It would never have occurred to anybody to even think of had I not done Konstantin in the same season as Edward II. So I love that.

What I feel is a great shame is that there are relatively few people in the same position as you.

I agree. Far too few. But I don't know whether this is necessarily the RSC's fault so much as the nature of the business that we're in now. It's up to the actors to say you are going to be doing acting hopefully for your whole life. It is worth spending time to learn to live, to be absolutely at home, to be **more** at home on the stage than anywhere else – and particularly on these big stages, doing these big plays. It's up to the actor, it's not up to the companies.

But I do hate the idea that we have in this country that somehow actors can live off the sheer grandeur of being a classical actor. I think some people in this country assume that's all one wants. It isn't good enough really, though I don't regret the fact that people regard the end of acting that I'm in as extremely posh. I don't mind that – it's just it's not **all** it is.

Is that a difficulty: that the RSC is regarded as something rather posh as opposed to something which everyone feels belongs to them?

I'd love it if people thought that. Funnily enough, the élitist question is not really evident when you see the audiences. We are probably less élitist than other art forms such as ballet and opera.

Do you like being able to see the audience?

No. I'm short-sighted and I don't wear contact-lenses is the simple answer to that, can't bear it. I do a lot of parts where I talk directly to the audience and I can't see a thing.

So what sort of sense do you have of them?

A very acute sense, obviously. I hear them cough, I hear them laugh and I get paranoid when I catch someone out of the corner of my eye who's sitting in a particular way which looks as though they're not interested. Occasionally you just glance at a scowling face or you hear a tut. On one famous occasion in Stratford, somebody shouted 'Rubbish!' at me when I was doing Ariel.

Do you get heckled much?

No. And I'm sure if I were more used to it I would be able to cope with it. I was so distressed when it happened. Which is pathetic actually, because I shouldn't be. That's what I do and absolutely I'm willing to listen to arguments against my performance – but if you're heckled there and then it's a very odd feeling. Because the way this production is conceived one can't turn round as Ariel, having spat in Prospero's face – which I agree was a vulgar thing to do – and give a long long speech about why I did it, because it ruins the exit. Horrible. Horrible, sick sick feeling.

I once heard a woman over the tannoy in the audience while I was putting on my make-up for the second half of *Ghosts*, and obviously the microphone was very near the woman because she said: 'I can't bear that Simon Russell Beale, I can't understand a word he says.' I switched off the tannoy very quickly and went on for the third act knowing – a very peculiar feeling – **knowing** that there was one person in the audience – and you didn't know who they were – who thought you were absolutely dreadful.

It's become a bit of a fashionable thing now that perhaps there should be more heckling – I don't know actually. I quite like the audience to acknowledge that thought has gone into it and therefore there should be channels whereby you can also express your disagreement with that thought. But to shout at the actors on the stage when they don't have the power to answer back is very cruel. I would prefer them to come round to the stage door afterwards and tell me: That was absolutely disgusting.

kathryn hunter
Just do it

Kathryn Hunter trained at RADA and won the Olivier Award
for Best Actress as Clara Zachanassian in Theatre de
Complicité's production of *The Visit*. This interview was
conducted while she was performing in *Pericles* at the Royal
National Theatre and about to start rehearsals for
Complicité's *Out of a House Walked a Man* . . .

Is acting something that you had to do, that you couldn't stop yourself from doing?

For as much a sense of: I must do this, there's nothing else I want to do, there's nothing else I maybe can do . . . in an equal measure there's doubt and fear.

Is the doubt and fear perhaps a necessary part of it? Would you still want to do it if that wasn't there?

I suppose the effect of doubt and fear on me is to make me want to work and clarify what I'm doing so that at least if ultimately I fail it's not for lack of work, of investigation. So it may be a good effect in that sense. But sometimes doubt and fears can be appalling, they can be really appalling because however much you tell yourself: It's only a play and dudududuuh, it's what you do, it's what you've **chosen** to do, it's what let's say between sixty and seventy per cent of your life is – and therefore if you're not happy within it, then you're slightly miserable however much you reason with yourself.

I suppose that factor, though, is one of the things which go towards making theatres places which can be very happy and warm and nice places to be: the fact that everyone who works there actually wants to be there. In comparison with other places where people work.

Yes, I think that initial experience of that first play I was ever in, *In the Jungle of the Cities* by Brecht at university . . . I don't think at the time I would have been able to pinpoint it but it was at the tech – I'd never been in a tech, I didn't know what a tech was – but watching designers, actors, the director, lighting designer, a whole group of people kind of converging on the same task, seemed really thrilling, that really caught me. And I suppose it is that that catches somewhere. You can have a day of doubt and fear and you go in and you meet the company for the evening's performance and something happens and you go: We're all in this together. That's good.

You went to RADA after university and obviously there is quite a long learning process in the acting profession – a lot of people say in fact that it never actually stops – but how much do you feel you can kind of quantify what you learn in terms of where it comes from and how?

It's very difficult, isn't it? The truth is that when I went to RADA, if I know very little now, I knew less than nothing then. All was to be learned. And they were very good, those teachers, movement teachers, some interesting directors and Hugh Crutwell was the leading light, from whom – unless I'm particularly stupid, I couldn't discern a particular philosophy – there wasn't a method as such, except a very large word, which was Truth. It's like reading the New Testament: the Kingdom of God is within you! It's the sort of thing you can ponder for the rest of your life. But it was invaluable. He knew what he meant and he recognised it and he would tell you if he didn't see it. And for me that was an extraordinary guidance. If there was a method he sort of plunged you in – his idea was jump in and learn to swim, learn by your mistakes: you can't just talk about it for ever and ever. And work with a whole variety of different people.

Then later one learned with other people. I worked with a company called Common Stock that was founded by Hattie Sullivan. She's researched over a lifetime methods used by Grotowski and Eugenio Barba. That was maybe the beginnings of a so-called physical theatre approach. Although the division is – as we all recognise now – not particularly useful.

And then with Complicité I went back to school again – to primary school! – because they actually do have a training. I find in my experience of working in British theatre there's a great instinct but there isn't a language of the body and of the space. There isn't actually a vocabulary for that feeling and I think Complicité and their training with Jacques Lecoq, they do have that.

British actors I think are able to pick up some sort of working relationship with each other much quicker than others that I've seen abroad.

Right. Because they're used to both moving very quickly and adapting very quickly.

I don't know if it's actually right to say that there isn't some sort of philosophy or any method or simply that it's never been articulated. Or that it's spread on a more unconscious level.

It does lead to: if there's less theorising, there's more sense of **doing** – you know, just get on with it. Don't talk about how difficult it is or how I do it, just do it. And I admire that. Because there is no single, **best** method – though personally I find if one can open oneself to different ways of performing it is both fun and enriching.

Max Stafford-Clark has his method, with the actions and things in, and I wanted to work with him to experience that. And I went with it and found it very difficult – but on purpose didn't question it, just to try it. Afterwards I felt that it has great value in terms of a clarity of thought that it results in on stage. Myself, I found that if used too early on in rehearsals it blocks. Because you pick up a play and you have a hundred and one instincts about it, but you shouldn't talk about or try and articulate or pinpoint them, you should just get up and do it and then do it again and then again. I find the action method useful if you're stuck or generalising, to say: Be more specific, what is your action here? But to try and fix those very early on, sitting down, where you're not in a physical relationship with the people you're going to be on stage with – it's a very forced relationship to decide your action like this. Your relationship here is to a book, whereas ultimately your relationship is in a space with the audience and with your fellow actors.

Are you encouraged, working within that system, to decide: That's the action – and then you have to stick with it? Or can you, the next day, say: Well I want to do a different action today, and then the day after that you can try something else.

Well, you can negotiate but the idea is that you agree in the end to play one. Maybe my mind is too chaotic – but I did find it very odd sometimes to play one transitive verb or one phrase or sentence because I think sometimes the way people behave, you know, they have multi-intentions in a moment, do you know what I mean, and to fix it on one . . . Maybe he meant that your main action, your main objective is that and around it you can have others, but I found it quite sort of stiffening in a way, it made me stiff. I used to have these transitive verbs rattling around in my head, rather than just engaging with the person. However, since working with him a couple of years ago, I do use actions, I think about what I'm doing, I think: That's very general, I don't quite know . . . What exactly am I doing? What do I want here? And I do go back and make myself find the actions. So in that sense I think it is a good method.

It's interesting as well that it's something that's come out of doing new plays. For a very successful and dense play it tends to be rather reductive because you're establishing a kind of skeletal alternative text to the text that's there – I think it would be quite tough to do a Beckett play that way. Having said that, I think for a slightly weak play with an interesting theme, strong scenes and rather saggy bits, sort of rather hacked together, the actions principle is probably rather a good way of holding that part of the show together and bashing through it . . .

The other virtue of it is that it is a way of binding a disparate group of people if they're all engaged in those actions and you're playing that game together. Only some people find it more painful than others! The clarity of thought is, I think, its advantage, it doesn't allow for fluffiness.

And I think as well, to be fair, the actors who have more second thoughts tend actually to be on top of it and want to get a bit more, rather than to be floundering and trying to catch up.

For me the constant in the years that I've been performing is not so much the relative merits of particular methods or ways of performing, it's been the question: What is the function of theatre? Does it have a function?

I remember seeing my first opera and there was a moment that was very wonderful. Before it people had been moving around in their seats, they were silent, but there are different qualities of silence, and then the lady singing touched a very true note about needing love or something like that – and the quality of silence in the auditorium changed completely. It was absolutely tangible. You could feel that collectively four hundred, five hundred people were attentive to what she was expressing in that moment and affected by it because it was very true and clear. It was a three-hour performance but that one moment and other similar moments when I've been in the theatre are what convince you that there are different forms of nourishment and that kind of spiritual nourishment is obviously a very important one.

I suppose the fact that we like to tell each other stories has the same origin. I mean, why do we do that? I have a twin sister and when we were eleven, we went to different schools. We used to religiously tell each other what had happened during the day – and then sort of invent little bits if it was quite a boring day. But there was this need to share your experience. I suppose somewhere I believe we need to experience, prompt other ways of thinking, other ways of feeling. And theatre is one of the last places we have left to do that.

I worked with Peter Greenaway a couple of years ago and he hates theatre. He finds it embarrassing to be asked to believe that the people on the stage are living this reality. But I think that's his problem. The magic of theatre is that most people come into the theatre totally willing and happy to suspend disbelief. They say yes, so and so is in a storm and his wife has died. They're happy to accept those premisses and go along with them and I think there's great joy in that kind of collectivism.

One of the things I do when I'm performing is try and imagine who is coming: that they've come, probably from work – maybe not – and they go through that foyer and buy a programme – or not – and then sit down. What are they thinking? What do they want? The great thing about travelling is that you do a play in front of very different people . . .

Do you feel that the reactions of most theatre audiences in this country are a true reflection of what the people feel – audiences in a number of other countries react in more demonstrative ways.

Oh yes. I remember we did a *commedia* piece with Complicité called *Help, I'm Alive!* and it was, you know, very large characterisations and very so-called physical playing. And in Brazil and Mexico the reaction was enormously voluble. I think the performance extended to ninety minutes. And when we played here at the Almeida, it came right down to an hour ten. There was lots of sex in it and the attitudes to all that were very different. They roared with laughter in Brazil and here the Almeida was quite – hm – pinched.

With *The Visit* and playing the Old Lady, people would say to me: What a monster! What a wicked woman! In fact people begin to think that **you** are like that. But when we played in Charleston in South Carolina they all thought that Clara Zachanassian was a heroine, they thought she was brilliant. She walks on and she says 'My God, what a dump' about the little town – in her furs and all that – and they thought this was hilarious. They loved her and they thought she was wonderful because she was stinking rich and powerful and vengeful.

Well that proves that the moral ambiguity of the play or the performance is working properly, doesn't it?

Yeah. It all comes from the text, all of it. The starting point is not a mystery, it's the text. Clara Zachanassian is said to be sixty-three years old, she's been plotting this revenge for fifty years, so she must feel quite strongly about it. She's got a wooden leg, an ivory hand, she married a very rich man, she's been used to having a great deal of money for a very long time and conducting her affairs as she wants. She drinks whisky and smokes cigars, which says something about her voice and her way of life; she has had seven husbands, which also says something about her level of willpower.

So there are all these givens in the text and from there you sort out how they affect you physically and then in each given situation in the play. You know: what's your pulse rate when you come back to the town that you left as a young girl of sixteen years old, that you were hounded out of and called a prostitute? And then you return fifty years later and you meet the man who betrayed you: what's your pulse rate at that moment?

So in terms of way of working, the starting point for me is always the text. And then building up a physical reality of the character. And of course the group of people who you're working with. With Complicité, in *The Visit* for example, there wasn't a sense of great psychological research, I mean I think we did that individually. There was much more of a sense of the dynamics of a scene and the dramatic climaxes of the scene. When they worked on the murder of Alfred III, they did I don't how many improvisations, there were a hundred different ways of killing him.

You were talking about putting together the physical manifestation of

the character and I wanted to ask you about costumes and at what stage that starts becoming important to you and how useful that is.

I think ten years ago it was absolutely normal for you to arrive on the first day, see the set, see your costume and off you go. Whereas now certainly I have been involved in a lot of productions where you have a dialogue with the designer, which I think is fantastically creative and fruitful.

For *The Visit*, Rae Smith was at rehearsals every day and she drew and drew and drew. And her drawings were fantastic provocations, because sometimes you don't realise what you do, you see something and you go: Ooh, you're right, I look like a spider there – OK. I'll use that image. When she first drew Clara in lime green trousers and a toad-like fur coat, I'd imagined something much more mundane but I went with it because of that kind of collaboration. We worked together.

I admire designers enormously, they can make or break a piece, as it were, really enliven it. However, I think there is a dangerous trend at the moment that in order to prove that there is a production value, there's got to be a certain level of glamour and show so that it looks **impressive**, for God's sake. You know I'm being trite but I wonder if economic pressures also play their part in that. When responses come, yeah, that was impressive, the wall came down and the floor went up or whatever, there's a danger that you're not actually serving the play but serving a kind of need to prove that it really is worth paying to the tune of £18.

Do you feel that the job that you do is an important one?

That's what engages me as a question. I don't know. But there are certain experiences that you have – I don't mean just when people come and relay what they experienced, but equally the times when you don't get any feedback but you just **know** that something has happened. And then I ride back home on my bike and I just feel **right**. Yeah, that's my function and I did it OK.

You might fall on your face the next day, but as long as those experiences happen with not too many gaps in between – where you know that something happened, there was a meeting point, a sharing with that theatre, that is enough confirmation for one to know: Yes it does have a function, being an actor, doing theatre.

Is there a theatre that you dream of?

I suppose my dream is of a classless theatre, of a climate where theatre increases in popularity, it becomes as popular as football, but there are hundreds of possibilities for how and where. As long as one keeps those doors open I think that's fine, it will go on happening.

michael pennington
Smoke and greasepaint

After a long association with the RSC, Michael Pennington
founded the English Shakespeare Company with Michael
Bogdanov in 1986, playing Prince Hal, Henry V, Bolingbroke,
Leontes, Coriolanus and Macbeth before leaving in 1992.
This interview was conducted while he was playing Claudius
and the Ghost in Peter's Hall's West End production of
Hamlet, a play in which he had already played Hamlet at
Stratford in 1980, Laertes at the Roundhouse in 1969 with
Nicol Williamson, and Fortinbras in Hall's 1965 production
with David Warner.

How did you start as an actor? Where did you train?

I didn't train. I was a university actor. I went from school into the National Youth Theatre for a time which had the unexpected effect of putting me on to the West End stage at the age of eighteen. There I was, as the Earl of Salisbury in *Richard II* just after my eighteenth birthday with a small soliloquy in the Apollo Theatre. So it was a bit headlong, the way I came into it – from school into that and from there to Cambridge, and I headlonged from that into the RSC because I was swept up as part of the supernumeraries to do *The Wars of the Roses*. It was like a battle campaign: during the two years that they did it there would be casualties, people would disappear, new recruits had to be brought in to play everything. This being in the days when there were companies of forty-five or fifty instead of half of that size. You were used pretty much as cannon fodder: Scene One Lancastrian soldier, Scene Two to change, Scene Three Yorkist soldier, Scene Four to change, Scene Five Lancastrian soldier . . . It was very difficult drawing a line for yourself, even with an actor's fertile imagination.

I think we were very fortunate. Looking back on it, it seems a comfortable series of choices to make.

Are you aware that the profession has become more difficult in the time that you've been in it, from a technical point of view? I don't mean employment circumstances or subsidy or any of that, but simply being on stage convincing people that you're real or that your character is real.

How can you act in the theatre in a way that's going to be more interesting than the telly or a movie – particularly for young audiences – is the crucial one here, I suppose. How do you stage fights in a way that is as convincing as in the cinema? And that really is a good thing for the theatre because it's forced people to design better fights, it's forced us to not accept certain conventions – whereby someone in a stage fight who gets kneed in the crutch has a remarkable tendency to get up and carry on fighting and all this business of making the napping sound and all that – I think we're more demanding about those things.

I suppose stage actors are always comparing themselves with movie actors. You find people in big theatres of fifteen hundred seats wishing to God they could do just that with their eyelid and make the point. And the fact is you can, in a way. Ian Holm was doing it in 1965 playing *Henry V* and *Richard III*. How to make a detail travel, how to make a small naturalistic detail travel is one of the great things in acting because it has to do with focus, you know: how do you make people watch, how you can move from an epic scale down to a very intense scale within the same minute?

Is there a sacrifice involved in playing, as we've just done, a four-thousand-seat amphitheatre in Athens? Well, obviously, being in a theatre which is not that brilliant acoustically, we found that you have to adopt a tremendously epic, physical, broad style of playing. In a way it was like being given a two-foot brush you would use for painting a wall and being asked to do filigree work with it. I wouldn't like to do it very often but it's nice to know it can be done.

What difference was there performing in the open air?

It was wonderful working under a sky. I'm a novice because I never played in the open air before, let alone in the middle of the night in Athens with the floodlit Parthenon just outside your line of vision. Characters in Shakespeare do frequently appeal to the gods or to God, usually in a sceptical way, like: Is anybody at home up there? To find yourself talking to an immense Greek night sky is certainly something quite different from looking up into the flying bars of a conventional theatre, there's something thrilling about it.

There are also things about those theatres which, without sounding too pious about it, certainly make you feel a connection with the roots of theatre. If Gertrude comes out to tell everyone about Ophelia's drowning and she's coming out of the central entrance in a Greek amphitheatre, talking to people who are in the orchestra down below, you realise it's exactly the same convention as the messenger coming out to tell everybody Oedipus's eyes have been put out. It's quite shocking because suddenly you know that the form is being used in a way that it has been used for two thousand years and elements of that form of story-telling are in Shakespeare too. So the whole thing is very interesting and exciting.

I think people are very demanding. They want you to be truthful. I don't think you can get away with anything. Why should you? I think people are quite quick to spot the sound and the fury and half-truths and generalisations. So I suppose it's true that the mechanical media have upped our game quite a bit in the theatre. People do expect a level of veracity and if they don't get it, even if they don't necessarily verbalise their dissatisfaction, there is a dissatisfaction.

Do you feel that this can sometimes make performances too small, too televisual?

I always think in terms of the classics when we discuss these things. If you're worried at all about how Shakespeare is done, you'd have to be concerned about the point at which understatement betrays the text of a Shakespeare which is after all highly formalised. Natural as it seems, the throwaway is not the best way of dealing with the constant pingpong of a Shakespearean text – or indeed the dynamic of a Shakespearean monologue.

The heroic style is rather distrusted now, and the ability to assess the geometry, say, of a Shakespearean monologue and develop it in a musical way, because it seems to be an artificial or an operatic concern. But you don't half get lost if you don't pay some attention to those values. You literally forget what you're trying to say if you let the thing die and take too many detours.

I remember doing a production of *Venice Preserv'd* at the National with Peter Gill a few years ago. That's a play which is written in huge speeches, there's not much stichomythia, it's all twenty lines – twenty lines, and there's always the natural instinct to interrupt or to go to interrupt or to provide a resistance to the person speaking and coming to the conclusion. It's not necessarily the best form of dramatic writing, Otway's, but in that form of theatre the best thing you can do is stay still until the other person is finished and internalise whatever you want to resist them with or to offer them because constantly you have the opportunity to interrupt and you don't interrupt.

To some extent that's true in Shakespeare as well, there are a lot of things it would be natural to do that it would not be helpful to do. So you're economising on naturalism when you're doing Shakespeare, it's not that you're becoming rhetorical but you're economising on what seemed an obvious thing to do because there has to be an overriding musical concern or dialogue concern.

I think one of the great attractions of the theatre is that you can also have uneven performances and somehow the theatre is a medium which forgives that much more easily than a film because there's always the possibility that some time in the next five seconds something will happen and everyone will click back in and click back in a bit harder for having sagged away.

Considering that we're supposed to believe in the suspension of disbelief and all this, being simply transported so that we didn't know the three hours had passed . . . I think we also know that audiences are constantly making judgements quite objectively on what they see, making comparative judgements about the actors in a play – Oh, he's not much good, but perhaps in a moment someone better will come on – and not being too disturbed about it. We dream of a production, particularly of a big classic, in which everybody's equally good and get terribly upset when a performance or a couple of performances in a production aren't working out so well. But I think audiences adjust for that all the time, they're surprisingly objective about those things, they'll say: I didn't like you when you did that, but when you did that it was very good.

In a way they rather like to be able to spot the difference—

Yes: That's the bit, he's the one, she's the one!

And they don't mind if someone then comes along and is better. But if it's all at a highly proficient level but one where you can't tell the difference in quality between one thing and another – which is often on the production team what you are trying to achieve!—

Absolutely, this is our dream of the perfect—

That's not necessarily as pleasing.
 Do you feel that there is or can be an underlying moral basis to

theatre, that it can have a meaning and resonance beyond showing off or entertainment or . . .

Yes, I do, but I think that you have to swallow the showing off and the entertainment element necessarily. You can't divide the one from the other and we all know, you know what a funny, tarnished but ennobling thing theatre can be both for the people in it and the people who experience it. But it is a notoriously difficult thing to talk about without sounding enormously pompous about something which is after all only smoke and greasepaint.

What I notice is that people still **go** to the theatre. I keep wondering who they are, particularly after doing so much touring: who are these people who come? It's not accidental. There is a **need** for it. And sometimes you try to relate that need to the state of a society. Under Thatcher is it more important for people to come to the theatre? Is it because they feel more starved than they would be under a more liberal Government, for example? There are all sorts of paradoxes about the thought that people only need the theatre when they're in desperate conditions in their lives. Those equations are difficult, but this funny tenacity of the theatre is what interests me.

I'm in a production of *Hamlet* at the moment which I suppose is why my mind is running so much on classics – but there is something about going to see *Hamlet*, there is an effect that that play has on an audience which is palpably different from any other play that I know. There's some sort of folk memory involved in it because usually people have seen it before and usually it has a special place for them and you're very aware that there are people seeing the play for the first time, very often in their early teens. You don't forget your first *Hamlet*. There is something very particular about that play and the nature of its effect on an audience.

I've been lucky enough to do a lot of Shakespeare and I know the occasional incredible satisfaction of doing those plays for an audience and the sense of feeling you've done a good day's work balanced with the terrible self-scrutiny and self-criticism and frustration. I remember playing *Hamlet* as being a really joyous experience most of the time, you knew that there was always something to develop, you knew that it was never **there**, it was never **it**. Something about being able to transmit the stuff in some way to an audience certainly does make you feel you're there for a purpose. And that's the best thing an actor can hope for. It's rare and it seems to happen more often with great plays like some of the Shakespeares or the Chekhovs for example: a real sense of why you're doing it, a sense of satisfaction about it. I also want to smear what I've just said by saying that of course it's also a load of silly showing off.

Most actors are genuinely in doubt as to whether what they do is important or not, whether it's hugely important, so that it becomes a kind of priest, or whether it is just a laugh or 'better than working' – you know, a means of getting drunk and sleeping with a lot of people that you might not get otherwise. All those things, all those versions of what the business is, most people are uncertain about and evade the question and privately think it's a bit of all of them.

Do you think that this uncertainty is one of the reasons why within the profession so few actors are in charge of their own destiny?

I do. I do exactly. And the fact that briefly I was I think is the exception rather than any form of rule. I think that uncertainty means you can't have the sureness of purpose that, say, a director or producer would normally have and I think that it's most unlikely for an actor to run a company. I don't think it's the actor's job, generally, to have an overview – I think the whole point of being an actor is to have an **underview** of it or at best a level view. And I think if you happen to be an individual who as well as enjoying your main work which is acting has a shadow running down the side of that activity which is a certain instinct for organisation or an interest in making things happen, I think that's unusual. If you have it you should take advantage of it. I took advantage of it for five or six years and now I don't want to take advantage of it ever again, I don't want to do it **ever** again.

And what are the reasons now that you don't want to do that any more?

Well, I feel, so to speak, the seam is exhausted. It was very wearing, just in terms of your stamina and your tolerance. It was bloody hard work and frequently very **isolating** work. It's not **quite** true what I'm saying because

I still want to poke about from inside projects that I'm in. I'm touring Shakespeare at the moment and have no managerial responsibility at all but I can't help having views about almost everything that happens and observing certain differences. I just can't keep my place, I keep wanting to interfere and having to stop myself – so that's the true answer to give you: it **is** sort of still there.

But I wouldn't want to take on the responsibility of getting those shows round the country and round the world, keeping a company sane and able to deliver, worrying about the money and all the rest of it and – worst of all! – trying to persuade people to give you money in this climate at the moment. Not at all. I wouldn't want to begin to try. And I think it's unlikely that actors do because I don't think we're naturally organisers.

I don't think actors generally are a political force. Most actors are happier in a kind of besieged mentality, you know, of hating the management, doing their work sort of in spite of the management and the sort of bravado that goes with that.

Was this an attitude you had to confront?

Yeah! It was rather odd. But I concluded that it was a **need** in actors to feel oppressed and to feel that there are people who don't understand and don't appreciate what they do. And that's part of the mechanism of doing it.

I always remember with the ESC, one of our great reforms was going to be open books and open offices and members of the company coming to board meetings – but none of them wanted to come. It was an invitation which wasn't taken up and was refused rather as if you were trying to sell the actors a pup, con them in some way. And certainly they didn't want to come, as if that would somehow compromise the integrity of hating the management if they found out how difficult it is to put anything on at all. There's a fear of complicating your thinking.

You see how I'm talking about 'they' already – I keep saying 'they do this' or 'they do that' – you see how odd it is that I should be talking about actors as 'they' at all.

But is that not also a feature of acting where you have to spend so much time thinking about your individual performance, what your body

is doing on stage, so the amount of solidarity, as it were, which exists in the profession is sometimes – even with the best will in the world – not that great?

No, actors in a group are brilliant at acting together and pretty much hopeless at anything else, I would say. What they're good at is relating to each other on the stage, usually in a rather generous way and with a very fine instinct for how the thing works, it's not just a matter of pushing yourself forward. I think the instinct to work as an ensemble is quite deep in most actors, good actors. But when it comes to attitudes towards the conditions in which they work or the significance of what they do or the issues of the day, most actors are very ineffective as a group even though individually they may be highly intelligent. It's an absolute axiom of touring that actors at an airport with a company manager in charge of them become like four-year-olds: we can't read the time our flight takes off, we can't read our boarding passes, we don't know which gate to go through without a nanny to show us. A most terrible group regression takes place. It may be true of all groups, not just actors. But the best group activity actors do is doing a play together, probably the only group activity they do . . .

What I'm saying is it's an absolute paradox: all actors want to take charge of things but very rarely go through with it for a good reason, that it's not on the whole a good idea.

How much does this apply to the rehearsal room and to the way that actors are encouraged to collaborate in the creation of the production and the performance by a director?

I've never been involved in the manner of Joint Stock with anything that's created by a group of actors more or less democratically, I've always worked in a more or less orthodox director–company relationship. So there's a whole area that I perhaps don't know about – though I assume that in groups somebody emerges as the director even if he or she is not called the director.

A group of actors is usually very quick to identify either a bad director or a director who's not being helpful in a genuine way, very quick to spot when something's wrong, very good at supporting each other and helping each other out of difficulties, very good at spotting when a costume is wrong – much more quickly sometimes than the designer or the director is. There's a kind of guild support system in a company in which people are very aware of how everyone else is getting on and whether the director is being helpful or not. Within a space of time of course that very often turns into a series of prejudices; the actors just bitch the director because he or she **is** the director or the designer, the whole thing becomes very generalised and rancorous if a company is less than perfectly happy. But the initial impulse is very authentic, very quick, and good usually, about what good theatre is. When an actor says: Actually you'd do much better if you were about a yard further away from her when you say that, or: If you don't touch him because then the suspense of the scene will be better sustained . . . often actors are much better than directors at spotting that sort of thing. A lot of directors have a strangely poor visual sense, for instance. Others have more visual sense than anything else. So that leads one to think that actors could take their destiny into their own hands. But I don't really think it's true.

Are there things that directors are good for?

Dividing and ruling. And of course at the best level absolutely creating the world in which the actors can best thrive. I do believe in the primacy of the director and I don't believe that it's a democratic process, I think there is a kind of autocracy involved.

I remember working with Lyubimov, it's a long time ago now but it was a very instructive time for me, ten years ago on *Crime and Punishment*, because he came in with a very, very particular way of working and a very particular idea of what he wanted out of the Dostoyevsky. And I know that because he's very, very forceful, the actors who did best with him were the ones who were prepared to abandon every aspect of the way they'd worked before if necessary and do it his way just for that one occasion. And that often involved copying what he demonstrated, for example, the thing that actors hate most of all: being shown how to do it by a director who also happened to be a very good actor. Very hard to accept, or at another level accepting that what he wanted out of you was fundamentally a message which was highly appropriate in Soviet Russia but might not be here because these codes are not so easily understood in England. He kept telling me to simplify

Raskolnikov. My English liberal humanist instinct was to make him a many-faceted person. He didn't want that, he wanted a murderer, an absolute . . . he wanted a villain. And he wanted a villain because he was saying something about the Soviet Union. So there's that tension, but with someone like that whose quality and whose nature you can sense very quickly it's best just to go with them. I mean, six weeks out of your life . . .

Maybe what I'm saying is that strength is the **point**, strength of purpose is the thing for a director. Because what's actually most alarming is a vacillating director, who doesn't seem to know why they're doing the play, what they want to do. That's when an actor's alarm signals go within the first few days and this sense of group activity starts going because people are desperately trying to save their backsides right from the beginning.

It's a tremendous thing to see the willingness of actors just to go and jump out of a plane without testing the cord, it's a very remarkable thing and is actually close to the centre of what an actor's strength is – that you can go from a production where you can be told to go three paces there, four paces to the left and speak in a high voice with the absolute willingness to do it and obey, and then to be in a production in which the director says: What would everyone like? and do that. The adaptability of actors and their willingness to trust the prevailing style – it's a willingness which is quite frequently betrayed or disappointed or frustrated – but the open-mindedness of actors towards different ways of working is I think very important, certainly in this country, and something to be proud of. It sometimes makes you look foolish, but it's a great thing to be willing to do.

Is that ultimately the great danger, every time you go out there, the idea that something may go wrong, more likely not your fault, and that you wind up looking a complete prat?

Certain things you're used to – the board going down, as it did two nights ago with us in Vienna. During the first hour of the play all the power went and we survived on an emergency generator for about half an hour until we got the power back. Those sorts of thing there's nothing to be said about, they happen. There are bomb scares and the whole splendid religiousness of the theatre performance is just abandoned by everyone. But everyone understands that – what's more alarming for an actor is the way in which he or she can screw himself up on a particular night, the sense of making wrong decisions on a particular night or being just way off form and relying on whatever carapace of technical efficiency and fundamental competence you have to get yourself through.

But the sense of not doing a good show is, for reasons which are hidden and personal – they're the most miserable nights that an actor has. Not for any lack of willingness, just you can be off form, like a sportsman, you really can. And then, for no reason at all, the opposite occurs and one feels **that**, one feels one's euphoria and satisfaction. You feel your own dissatisfaction in the same way, more than any external disasters, not measuring up to what you think you can do. It's not the usual matter of absolute public disgrace, more a sort of sour feeling of not having done too well for yourself and whatever private muses.

It must be quite a difficult situation when you're working in a group and this is happening to someone else.

The instinct is first to curse them for letting you down. And then soon after that to want to help them out of their own difficulties. But no actor knows what the whole of another actor's evening is like. They only know the bits that affect them, the bits they're on with them in, and you certainly notice if somebody has either suddenly gone quiet or has gone **slow** above all. It's a mixture of annoyance and sympathy that one feels about that.

Having spent most of my days in repertoire theatres, I don't like long runs but I do like continuous runs. You can't half build – because you remember exactly what happened twenty-four hours ago, when it is that something isn't working any more and why it is that something's not working any more. You get a chance to be quite craftsman-like because the memory is so fresh, and you have an immediate opportunity to get it right or to change it or develop it in some way. Beyond three or four months a whole different set of problems to do with staleness may well come in. But I rather like the conventional run.

How do you prepare yourself before going on?

I've got no great dogmas about that. Some people come two and a half hours early. Irving used to come in two hours early – until he met Ellen Terry who taught him how to be late. She said: No, no, no. **Rush** down the stairs onto the stage and you'll act much better. And he did! Before, he used to stand there in the wings for an hour giving his performance before he went on – rather stilted. And she taught him that precious rule to be running against time. So out he went fresh. There are some lovely paradoxes about this sort of thing. A load of things you would think would be true are not true – you don't have to be thinking about the bloody play all the time all through the day to do it well, possibly the reverse.

Is this true of afterwards as well? Can you just leave it, walk out the door, get on with the rest of your life?

Yeah, I think so. You need a drink. No question. You need a drink and you probably want something to eat, you need to let rip a bit. You can also still be there half an hour after the curtain comes down going: Christ, that's unbelievable. Either way is OK. I find there are few rules about it. If you knew what the rules were it would be easy.

And less fun probably as well.

Absolutely.

patrick marber

A laugh every twenty seconds

Patrick Marber spent several years as a stand-up comedian before gravitating towards radio and television. He co-wrote and performed in *The Day Today* and *Knowing Me, Knowing You* for BBC TV. His first stage play, *Dealer's Choice*, premièred at the Royal National Theatre in February 1995.

To me, stand-up comedy is the ultimate in live performance because it's just you and an audience. The extreme vulnerability of that makes me feel that any live performing I do now could never be as frightening.

It's interesting that it's something for which there's no training.

No. To do it for the first time is the most strange, bizarre experience. Most things you can relate to something else: it was like this or that experience – but it's like nothing else. But the weird thing about it is how quickly you develop an immunity to it and how quickly it becomes second nature to go on stage as yourself and talk about yourself or funny things that have occurred to you and it **not** seem strange.

But this isn't really the same self.

Of course, a stand-up's persona is always a version, an exaggerated party-time version of him- or herself. It's yourself when you're being particularly interesting – one hopes. One of the reasons I actually stopped doing it was I became – I'll have to choose the word carefully – I became . . . No, I won't choose the word carefully – I got pissed off with pretending to be myself when I knew that this was not how I actually was. And it seemed to me ironic that although you are yourself as a stand-up comedian, you know that you are very much not yourself and it seemed like a ludicrous lie in the end.

I became more interested in developing characters comically and I started working with Steve Coogan and doing *The Day Today*, stuff like that, which was more character-based. And I felt much more at home writing for other people and writing characters for myself than I did writing jokes for myself.

It's one of the interesting things actually about single stand-up comics compared with a situation where there are more people, where it's more akin to acting, even if it's just a double act. If you think of double acts like Laurel and Hardy, then the two of you are always able to play off each other and in a way sculpt the stage characters around the other one, accentuating particular differences between you. You can give a character certain sympathetic qualities and certain unsympathetic qualities. I feel it's quite important to always have one sympathetic

character on stage – and when you're doing it by yourself that means it's got to be you. You have to be in some way likeable.

Actually I'm not sure that you have to be likeable, I think you have to be interesting. One of the best stand-ups in my view was Gerry Sadowitz who was an unlikeable persona. But I know what you mean: you have one relationship and that's with the audience and the problem with stand-up on the cabaret circuit is that you have twenty or twenty-five minutes to develop that relationship with an audience so it can't be a particularly complicated thing.

I think if you see a stand-up doing their own show, doing two hours, if you go and see someone like Billy Connolly, you'll see a complexity of character and it's obviously much more fully developed. But I never graduated to anything longer than about half an hour because I couldn't come up with the gags, basically. And on stage you have to get a laugh every fifteen, twenty seconds or else you're sunk.

Do you feel a real pressure about that?

As a stand-up? Absolutely. Some people find it a breeze, you know, people like Jo Brand, Jack Dee, who are people I know quite well. They seem to have no problem sustaining a persona, coming up with the material, being interesting. It's not a problem to them because that's what they're **naturally** good at. It wasn't what I was naturally good at. I had a facility to do it but it wasn't where I really belonged. And it took me three or four years to learn that – and thoroughly enjoyable years. But I was never one of those comics who loved being on stage making people laugh, it didn't actually give me a kick at all, it was just a blur of anxiety. Whereas you feel with some people that they **need** to be on stage, that's where they feel most at home.

Somehow, if they couldn't do that—

Exactly, it would be a deprivation. But a day when I had a gig would be a lost day because it was just pure fear for the whole day.

Did you have a particular preparation ritual?

Absolutely not. I would try very hard not to think about **anything**. All day. And walk on stage with no preconceptions about anything. I had technical preparations in that at one time I did an act where I had quite a few props. So I'd have to prepare this little briefcase with all my toys in it and that was quite nice, to have something to concentrate on, like an actor preparing their props or putting on a stunt show or whatever.

And I'd always watch the show and see where the trouble was in the audience if there was any and see how the audience were playing. And look to see if anybody was doing the same joke that I was about to do.

Do you feel very proprietorial about your jokes?

Oh yeah. I think all comics do. If you saw someone doing something that you thought: that's nicked – you'd go bananas. Because it's **your** joke.

Has it stopped you from nicking anybody else's jokes?

I've never knowingly nicked a joke. Of course subliminal nicking does go on. But no – that is the cardinal sin. I think it's the main distinction between what is absurdly called the alternative circuit and the mainstream circuit – the alternative **is** now the mainstream, but that's another thing altogether. I think in the olden days material was a movable feast in a sense because comics were much less a persona and much more about gags and controlling an audience. And I would say the older-style comics are probably technically more competent than the newer people because they've worked rougher venues and they know more jokes.

The modern lot are much more concerned with projecting a notion of personality, of: This is my view of the world, this is my little angle on life . . . Because they have to find something that makes that distinct. It's not that different from the cliché of comedy as the new rock 'n' roll. All clichés have a grain of truth in them and I think people say that because quite a lot of it now is about image. You have to, in a short space of time, project what your selling point is, your angle: oh yes, you're the comedian who makes surreal observations about this fridge – and you're the one who makes aggressive observations about the Government, or whatever. People need a pitch now.

I read somewhere, can't remember where, that audiences are only interested in taking from the performers, they don't give anything. Do you think that's true?

No, I think audiences at a comedy show want to have a good time, they want you to be funny – and they'll give you about twenty seconds to prove that you are. Then if you're not you're dead.

They haven't gone there to tell you that you're funny, though. They're out there waiting to have done it for them.

Any audience is out there subliminally saying: Come on, show me what you've got. But they want you to show them something good. So at the start of any performance, it's nil–nil but you're playing at home. If you perceive the audience as the enemy (which of course they **are**, but you can't perceive them as such), then it's difficult. You have to give them the benefit of the doubt.

Is there a particular place where you felt there was always an especially good audience?

I like performing in a little pub in Islington very near to where I live, it's a pub called the Market Tavern: little basement, very hot and sweaty. I could walk to the gig. It was always good to be able to walk to work. I could arrive two minutes before I went on stage, walk on stage, do my act, piss off and be home two minutes later. It was wonderful. And because I was always in a good mood about doing that gig, I always had a nice time there. And, you know, because the audience are from my neck of the woods – I like working locally.

What do you do after the performance?

If I'd done a good performance I'd swan around, talk to people. If I did a bad performance I'd walk off the stage and into the car. There was no way – I'm not going to stay in that room. Sometimes I wouldn't even pick up my money. I'd say: Thank you very much, good night, **send the cheque**. I'm off, I'm out, I'm gone. But a good performance, the most pleasurable thing for me as a stand-up was, having done a funny performance, being able to relax for about two or three hours with the other comedians, having a drink, go for an Indian and bask a bit.

I wouldn't want to say that I don't enjoy performing live, it's more that I don't **need** to perform live. If I never performed live again it wouldn't bother me. It would bother me to never perform again. I like putting a 'tache on and swanning around. But to me the performing side of things is easy, because I find writing so hard and inevitably if you find something quite simple to do, you're either not very good at it, which I concede is a possibility, or you're not so concerned about it that you get all worried.

Is the dressing-up element and the idea of being a different person – and convincing other people that you're that different person – one of the major attractions?

Absolutely. And doing *The Day Today* and *Knowing Me, Knowing You* where I get to do a range of characters and I don't have to be that person night after night for six months, it's absolutely ideal for me: I have the pleasure of creating the character, I have the pleasure of performing the character and then I have the pleasure of **not** being the character. That's perfect.

I've always thought that one of the toughest things about being a stage actor is that you invariably will get cast along particular lines because of your physical make-up. If you look like a Hamlet, you stand a chance of getting cast as one, if you don't look like one that makes it very tough for all sorts of reasons which may have nothing to do with your acting ability or your understanding of the character. It must be quite a tough mental struggle adjusting to that.

It's horses for courses. I'm never going to be Hamlet. I might make it to Malvolio one day. And you have more time as Malvolio to piss about backstage, you know . . . it's OK. I've always felt from the first part I ever did, which was Androcles when I was about ten or something, very early on I think an actor decides what their range is, and I think that their body tells them what their range is. That's life and yes, it's unfair. But who ever said it was fair? I don't think it's a bad thing. It's a bad thing if you're twenty-five and you want to be something that you can't be, but that's for each actor to cope with. Then again there are people who redefine your notion of what a type is: you know, Woody Allen is a romantic lead . . .

Though his parts are always built around the paradox that he's the romantic lead—

He also wrote them, so that helps. You'd be pretty stupid if you wrote yourself the shitty part.

When you're a performer and you're in trouble, where can you look for help?

As a stand-up? Oh, the compère – you just get off. Again it depends entirely on the context. If you're doing your own two-hour show and after ten minutes the audience aren't laughing, then you need to address that situation, because you're stuck with them for two hours. In a twenty-minute set, if the audience aren't laughing after ten minutes, you can cut it short. It varies. But often I've done gigs where the audience weren't laughing and then someone heckles and I've managed to deal with the heckler in a funny way and got the audience back on my side. That can happen, when something live occurs that changes the dynamic of the performance to your advantage. Also it can change to your disadvantage: I've had shows where I've been going very well, audience have been laughing, someone heckles in a jolly way and I've come down on the heckler like a ton of bricks and killed the atmosphere. It's a very fragile thing: you can think that you're the boss and then someone can just upset it all, it's so subtle. And it's just something that you get better and better at.

If you go and see someone like John Hegley, his ability to control atmosphere in a room is superb. He's by far the best live cabaret performer around. He's streets ahead of anybody else and that's because he's been doing it a very long time and he's just supremely confident, supreme technically – he doesn't need a director because he's worked it, he's just on top of it. But he's a rare example.

He's someone who's been a hero of mine for years and years and to me he's comically, technically, artistically, in a different league. Because I think he actually presents a vision of the world. He can make people laugh, he can move people – he does something *dramatic*, he changes the nature of the room that he's in. If you see him on a bill with lots of other people, he won't necessarily get the most laughs but, for me, he'll have the most effect. And that's really what it's about. It's not the act who makes people laugh the most, it's the act who comes on and changes the nature of the evening.

Would you be reluctant to follow him on a bill?

Hegley? Well I wouldn't because I'd never be in that position. Because he'd always be top of the bill, fortunately.

Is there a danger – I think a Woody Allen character suggests this at some point – of an audience getting laughed out?

No, I don't think that's true. I think there's always laughs **left**, but it's the kind of laughter that's left. But again someone like Hegley, he's a master of that. He can follow someone who's brought a house down and he will change the nature of how he performs. So he might start by not trying to get many laughs but just by trying to control the situation, establish his presence as being different from that that's been before. And then, once he's got control of the space, to start to take people into his way of doing things. He thinks about the way each piece of material should be presented, so that it isn't just the same way of presenting things, he's constantly looking for new things: slides, music, puppets . . . He's very, very rare.

john hegley
Georges Braque & Johnny Rotten

One of the comedy circuit's most enduringly popular acts,
John Hegley is a poet, musician, singer, graphic artist and
performer. He is a regular contributor to *The Guardian* and
has published four books of poetry, *Glad to Wear Glasses,
Can I Come Down Now, Dad?, Five Sugars Please* and
These Were Your Father's, and released one CD,
Saint and Blurry.

The first theatre work you did was in children's theatre. How did this come about?

The first job was at Interaction and I was taken on initially as a musician/actor. They did plays outside, in adventure playgrounds and parks. And it was a game play – Ed Berman had brought the game play style of doing stuff over from America with enormous participation, everybody sitting in a circle with the kids around them, and games in the play. I enjoyed that aspect of it very much, the participatory element, and from that day it's never left the show that I do, there's always that game element in the performance. I did that for three months – it was a summer scheme – and it was my first experience of performance and of money: £3.50 a week plus 50p a day, dinner subsidised. That was '78. I left there and joined Soapbox theatre in '79 or '80. That was again a kids' company, again out in parks, but more formalised in that the kids would sit in front of us and we would act the play out to them. Both times I had a hand in writing the stuff.

Do you think audiences of children were good training for dealing with adult audiences?

Oh yeah.

What are the differences?

Generally adults will be more controlled, even when they're drunk, **generally**, than a group of undrunken children. Children tend to be drunk on themselves, the noisy ones, and that's usually more difficult to deal with than people who are drunk on alcohol. I remember a drama advisor in Redbridge – I think his name was Alan Black – saying you don't have to get the kids to physically join in to participate, they can participate **emotionally**, which I always thought was a very good point. Maybe sometimes we didn't bring that side of things up enough in the shows, though I think subsequently Soapbox went on to make much more emotional involvement with the kids. It was really good to be told that.

You get more ego gratification with adults, but you get a lot of spiritual gratification with kids. So that's why it's good not to stop doing the kids' stuff. Though you get spiritual gratification with adults sometimes, when people come up and say: You made me laugh, I've been feeling bad.

When did you start doing the stand-up stuff?

In '81. That was the Comedy Store and there was this wrestling with the audience a little like you do with children, which took a while to get good at, but once I knew how to play it I quite enjoyed the wrestling with them.

And what made you want to work on your own rather than in a group of people?

There is an element of choice in it but doing poetry – it tends to be something that one does as one. One is one and all alone. But **not** ever more shall be so. I did a play on Radio 4 recently, that was an ensemble piece and it was a joy to do that. It was really good to work in an ensemble again.

I'm interested in that moment when you're in the play with a group of people and there are moments when you're not on. You can be off stage and yet it's going on without you, it has its own existence but you're still part of it.

I was never off stage. I was in every scene. But in the next play, there's one scene where I'm not in it. It's tiny but it's a bud, isn't it?

A friend of mine runs a class at the City University called Serious Comedy and he gets people to come along and talk about their side of things. And I went along and read that out and then got them to do it and got somebody to play me. And this was amazing. I sat down and there were four people doing this thing . . .

It must be rather strange to see somebody play you.

It was a bit like astral projection.

Can you remember when the Comedy Store started – was there a

feeling that here is a new kind of theatre that's closer to the audience and what we're interested in and what we want to do?

I suppose we didn't really think of it in terms of theatre. Certainly Rik Mayall, Nigel Planer, Peter Richardson and Adrian Edmundson, those four were very much theatre, I thought. But it's quite hard to take theatre out, and make it stick its claws in rather than let you come to it, as much as you had to there with drunken people who were gonging people off. I think they would say, all of them, they were actors rather than stand-up comics. And I suppose I was then more of a stand-up comic than an actor, although not quite – because I was singing and doing poems, so it was different, it was performance rather than acting. And I suppose I got pleasure out of doing good metre with a poem about a farting dog. I thought: The metre in this is good and I'm glad you're getting good metre, you're getting good rhyme schemes and good wordplay.

That period and the period just before was when punk happened and on the back of that the huge diversification of independent labels. Many people were suddenly realising the possibilities of expressing themselves in new forms, in ways which were very different from and in many cases a lot more personal than the sort of products one had previously been offered. And yet that never really seemed to happen in the theatre, certainly not in the organised, play-going theatre.

Ever hear of the Demolition Decorators? They were from North London, some of them had been involved in Interaction, and they used to do happenings and hand out bits of hoover to the audience. They would have songs, bits of hoovering and then they painted the audience. They had that anarchic element in their theatre – but they were the only ones. I used to love them. They used to have this Swami at the Glastonbury. He was called the Swami and he sat in front of a television screen and then he had a big piece of polythene and candles all lit up and he sat all day in front of the television with all his acolytes, women dressed in white.

I'm interested in theatre and I have some understanding of the tradition and what can be done with it and I like to see experimental stuff. I saw a thing called *The Masterwork* at the Riverside in '81 that was absolutely

Vanessa Redgrave, Young Vic

Max von Sydow, Old Vic

Linda Marlowe, Old Vic

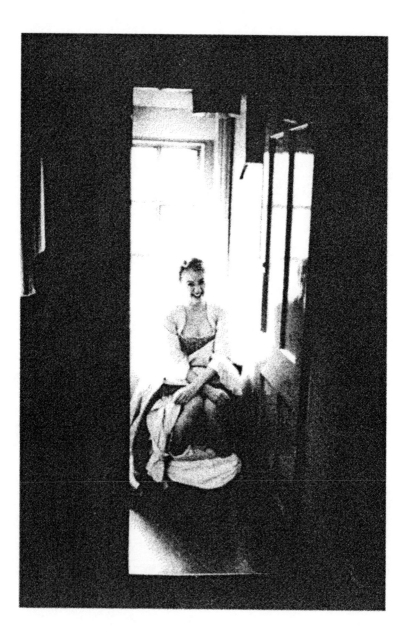

Niamh Cusack, Old Vic

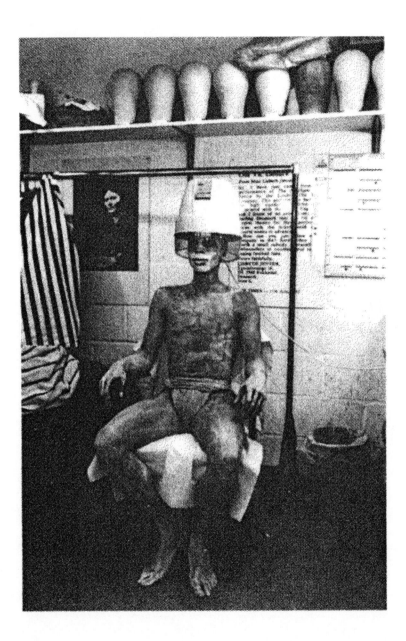

Cyril Nri, Old Vic

Michael Gambon, Theatre Royal, Haymarket

Billie Whitelaw, Riverside Studios

Anthony Hopkins, Royal National Theatre

fantastic, a multimedia thing with great big lumps of stone in there, forklift trucks and people doing acrobatics, but the acrobatics second to the dramatic action and that really blew me mind.

So I try to keep a theatrical component in. And when I go round art galleries, it always makes me think: you should get a **set**! And you should have a set that is **ambiguous**, because you come on and you're relatively unambiguous. I like the element of ambiguity.

But that's when you start working with other people, when you're into an exciting area. How exciting it must have been to have made that *Masterwork*, which really did work masterfully. It was a brilliant, brilliant piece. It would be good to get some more people involved.

I suppose you belong to the first generation of stage performers who grew up listening to rock music and being inspired by musicians. Indeed, you are a musician. Do you feel this has a bearing on the kind of experience you want to see in the theatre when you go and what you want to offer people when you're up there?

In the sense that I want it to grab me, to get hold of me. But then the other part of it is like Georges Braque – a combination of him and not necessarily Johnny Rotten but somebody like that, the two: the beautiful, ambiguous image and the throttling, arresting gesture. That's what we're after. Basically I need to get Georges Braque along to paint my set for me.

You use a lot of music in your performances – do you think that's useful in offering a different set of tools for addressing the audience?

My girlfriend said she thought the musical bits were just a break where you didn't have to listen so much, which was a bit of a shock. Hopefully it's not going to be so much like that. I'm just working out a new show for Edinburgh and there are less songs in it – there's six songs in about an hour: twenty-five per cent to a third will be music.

They feel good for **me**, I suppose. Maybe they give me a break, that's an important point. Because it's quite hard coming out . . .

I think to be fair it's a lot more than a break because songs are related

to rhythm and time and they're very effective in changing a mood or an atmosphere and creating a different situation. And I think if it's a fast song, people's pulses do start going slightly quicker, they do wake up and are prepared to start reacting in a more engaged way. And if they're maybe too jittery, something soothing will calm them down a bit, prepare them for something more truthful, possibly. So I think it's a very useful component of what you do. And I think it's quite sophisticated.

I think it's having too many songs in a block. The way you're describing, the song is a transition to the next phase, *Pennies from Heaven*-style. And that's how I'm trying to work it this time. This is the first time I've ever really structured the show because this is the first time the show is more of a thematic continuum. It is all related to love and relationships. It goes more or less chronologically through a whole series of relationships, from my first relationship with my first puppet pet animal to the most recent relationship. Although it's to some extent fictional – or, should I say, not so much fictional as some steps removed from reality. The music is in there – it's definitely much more integral.

I do think it's a great loss to British playwriting that somehow the musical is despised as a frivolous form and somehow one which doesn't quite address—

Well Potter changed all that didn't he?

He should have done. But if you look at what people are writing for the theatre, it's all very hung up on the power of the word.

He changed it as a possibility, I mean.

Are you very conscious when you're writing that what you write is going to be something you will have to perform?

I write about the experience that I haven't retrieved from my memory – and I discover as I write. Then you fictionalise it as well, where necessary, and not fictionalise it sometimes as well, even though you might make a bigger joke. I wrote this story about being in this relationship and people were finding it painful. And I thought: I don't want you to find it painful, wincing at the suffering that I was undergoing on this journey. It's no good, I don't want you to feel it that acutely or that really. So I've put in some fabrication to make people think: It can't **really** be true. Which is a very interesting reason to put in absurdity.

I really think this is an interesting area I've arrived at now. And new for me. It is more dramatic, what I'm doing. This is the joy of performing what you do – because I wouldn't have discovered that if I'd been writing a play. It would have gone out and you don't make changes like that, generally, it's not such an organic thing. It's definitely stretched to: This may not be true. And hopefully: This is funny. Not: This is just tragic, but: This is funny and it is tragic! This is Braque and Johnny Rotten! This is comedy and tragedy! This is dual!

A lot of people have said that comedy only ever comes out of pain or some kind of suffering, that there is a price to be paid for it at some point along the line. Do you think that's true?

It's not always based on suffering, it's sometimes just based on stupidity. But outside those two there's probably not very much.

What experience would you like the audience to have when they see one of your shows?

Joyful, healing, wounding and hilarious.

Why wounding?

The other side of the coin, really. Maybe wounding before healing – I put them the other way round – because you've got to go down to go up. No you haven't got to go down to go up, that's false, but if you go down **first**—

You can go up higher and you know you've been there as well.

But there we are: grandiose aims!

Otherwise you wouldn't be doing it, would you?

No.

Can you imagine a life where you weren't performing?

I can imagine it. No. It wouldn't be a good idea. I'm better at performing than I am at certain other aspects of living so it's better for my morale that I do something that I do alright.

ian saville
Socialist conjuring

Magician and ventriloquist Ian Saville performed his first solo
show, *Brecht on Magic*, over six hundred times. This was
followed by *Getting Nowhere – Again*, with William Morris,
and *Left Luggage*, which he was busy rehearsing at the time
of this interview.

In 1978 I joined a theatre group called Broadside Mobile Workers' Theatre which was an offshoot of Red Ladder. But we were more Left. Red Ladder had gone up north to Leeds and taken the name. We had the ladder, we had the ideology. We kept very strictly to the principle of workers in struggle and we went into occupations and picket lines and all those sort of things. That's a very interesting performance situation, performing to a group of workers who are occupying a factory, where they have taken over this place they have been working in and now see it in a completely different way. The group saw my magic tricks as a good asset, for getting people laughing to begin with and for getting the atmosphere nice and jolly before we went in with the heavy political stuff.

And what was the reaction to the heavy political stuff?

It seemed generally to work OK, but there were all sorts of other problems within the group in terms of internal politics and structures and criticising ourselves. I mean we operated a labyrinthine process of criticism and self-criticism and quarterly assessments and individual self-assessments – and then people coming in and criticising you for what you'd missed out while criticising yourself – all that sort of thing. I was judged not to come up to the standards of the group eventually. I was reorganised out of it.

Did this have anything to do with the magic tricks?

Partly. There was a feeling that I hadn't devoted enough attention to making my magic tricks as **radical** as they should be. I argued at that time it was actually impossible to make magic tricks more didactic and explanatory about the world because in the process of doing a magic trick you hide the way things work – so there's no correspondence between what is actually happening there and the theoretical idea that you're trying to put forward. But that was a rather weak excuse.

Eventually, after I left the group, I developed the magic tricks more, trying to incorporate the socialist ideas into them. That was when Rock Racism and the Anti-Nazi League were starting up and I started doing magic at some of their gigs.

Can you give me an example of that?

The classic example is the trick with the three pieces of rope which are different lengths. I developed it to be an illustration of the three different classes in society. They change and become the same length – and the audience applauds at that point. But I stop them – because there are still classes. The process has to continue until eventually I get one piece of rope which is a classless society. That developed quite early on. And it was always slightly tongue-in-cheek. It was playing about with ideas, which I think was the appeal of it, but in a way that wasn't hostile to the ideas.

It's interesting that these very traditional theatre forms suddenly start to become very fashionable again.

I am always looking for ways of incorporating old things in what I do. In the latest show I have quite a lot of very unconventional ventriloquist's dummies, they're not the normal sort of thing that you associate with ventriloquists. That came partly from looking at ventriloquism in the nineteenth century. This thing of having a single ventriloquist with one small dummy comes from the late music-hall era. The cheeky chappie crosstalk act developed quite late. It's been the dominant thing in this century – but before that ventriloquists generally had lots of large dummies on the stage and they would act out a scene running between all these people rather than just having a crosstalk act with one.

So it's more like a puppet show?

I think the question of lips moving or not was less important. Although actually it's never been all that important in ventriloquism. The most successful ventriloquists have been the ones who've been on the radio: Edgar Bergen in the States and Peter Brough and Archie Andrews in Britain.

Did television distort that by making it more of a technical exercise, rather than entertainment?

Yes, although it was exploited then by people like Arthur Worsley who did this act where he didn't speak at all and the dummy kept challenging him to say things. That's where the 'bottle of beer' phrase comes in because the dummy keeps shouting at Worsley and insults him the whole time saying: I bet you can't say 'a bottle of beer', you can't say 'a bottle of beer', can you? A bottle of beer, a bottle of beer, a bottle of beer! And it builds up into a crescendo as you realise that this is the dummy saying 'a bottle of beer' while Worsley's sitting there, deadpan face, taking all this, not coming back at him. It's a beautiful position that the audience is put in.

I started developing ventriloquism because I thought that was a good way of introducing Bertolt Brecht into my act and that's when I devised the longer show, moving on from the cabaret act and making it more of a theatrical show with a plot. The basic plot was that I was a socialist magician and I was going to tell the audience how I'd become a socialist magician. And that was by introducing this Bertolt Brecht dummy.

Could you perhaps explain the theory of socialist conjuring? The way I remember it is that capitalist conjuring is about tricking people, it's about cons, it's about deception. But socialist conjuring gives you the deception but also the explanation.

Yes, it's using mystification to demystify people about the world. I start off by showing people the difference between a socialist conjuror and a bourgeois conjuror by showing the bourgeois conjuror doing a trick in which a red handkerchief turns blue. And I decide to do the dialectically opposite method of subverting this trick – and in the process I make the blue handkerchief turn red and go through the motions of showing the audience how it's done. But in fact they don't see how it's done. So there's a bit of playing with the audience about the nature of the fact that they're being fooled on one level, but on another level I'm telling them real things that I believe are true about the world. So they're not being fooled.

I tend now to be aiming less for, you know, getting people to go out and change the world immediately after the performance than I think I was at one time. It is much more complex than that and I think the process of seeing things happen in front of you, the performance arena in itself, is more important than I had maybe given credit for in terms of thinking about political theatre. There's a danger in thinking about theatre related to political action that you think of the important thing happening after the theatre has finished. But what happens in front of you, what is actually happening there with the audience, is the thing that interests me most, the way in which people enjoy and are stimulated by performance at the time.

And is this reinforced by your own experiences as someone in an audience seeing other people?

Yes, I think it is marginally, yes. What I get out of seeing performances, what I enjoy most about that process is the sense of heightened being that you get from performance, that actually being there in that place and enjoying it and being with other people and sharing their ideas.

Have particular magicians inspired you?

The ultimate comedian magician of course was Tommy Cooper. I saw him live when I was fourteen at Bournemouth. He was absolutely amazing and he was an inspiration to me, the level of humour, the level of playing with an audience, but he did it without any self-analysis or thinking about it, it was just an amazing ability to be here and now and to manipulate an audience without thinking about it.

I remember when I was young seeing an American magician called Tony Slydini – I went to a sort of club for young magicians at that time – he came over and did some close-up magic. He's sort of acknowledged by magicians as being one of the experts on misdirection and actually doing what is the **real** magic. That really did impress me a lot.

I think what he does is very interesting for actors as well in terms of understanding about how an audience's attention works and how one's own attention works. The central thing in magic is misdirection which is, when you start looking at it, very similar in some ways to some of the things that Stanislavski was talking about, it's looking at him from a different angle. The circle of attention for the actor is similar in some ways to the way in which the magician manipulates the direction of attention of an audience. I think there is a lot to be learned from the way in which magicians approach an audience. They have to be conscious of the naturalness of movement and reproduce it while doing something else at the same time. It's not a question of – as people think – the quickness of the hand deceiving the eye, it's the naturalness of the movement. It's being able to observe how people do things in real life: How would you hold a card in this situation? Because if you do it slightly differently, the audience will know. Even though you have to do something else at the same time. So you have to observe those details very closely – which are important to actors as well.

The question of magicians revealing their secrets is an interesting one too. I suspect when people tell you they're revealing the secrets they may not be – it's a different, more refined trick. And in a way this leads on to what I wanted to ask you about your relationship with other magicians. Whether people do go around and see each other's acts and sort of try to adjust their acts and develop them as a result?

Oh yes. The magic world is strange in a way in that most of the members of the Magic Circle are not professional magicians. It's a hobby world to quite a large extent and a lot of the people who do magic and get very, very good at it wouldn't dream of ever going on stage and performing – certainly not as a career. So magicians do share ideas and moves and bits of things that you can do with bits of equipment. There's also quite a commercial set-up in terms of sellings tricks as well to people at quite high prices.

So how much does a trick cost?

Well, people can pay thousands and thousands. A lot of the most effective things I do are very simple, cheap things. The magic trick that I do that attracts most wonder is where I tear up a newspaper and restore it to one piece and that's something that I got from a particular book and I remake every time. I don't give it away. But it's something that's very cheap and certainly one of the most effective tricks that you can do.

The thing that magicians often neglect is the performance aspect. It's very easy to get carried away into making the things more and more elaborate instead of thinking about: What is the plot of what I'm doing? What is the story that's going to interest people? Houdini's skill in doing his escapes was not at the centre of his theatrical gift. It was the fact that he could find new challenges and set up a dynamic with an audience. Not just the audience in the theatre but the public at large – all these elaborate challenges, saying: I'm going to challenge the police force in Britain, you can find the most difficult cell for me to get out of in Scotland Yard! Creating that drama was much more unique than the technicalities of how he did it. Generally I'm not all that in favour of giving away how the tricks are done.

I'm not asking you to.

I know, I'm just explaining why. Because anybody who really wants to find out can find out. I have a different attitude to people who come up to me after I've performed and say: Oh, I wish I knew how that was done. I won't explain the trick to them, but sometimes kids come up to me and say: I'd like to do magic and I'd like to find out how things are done, how can I find out? And then I tell them which books to go and look at and so on.

So you feel the extremity of the trick, the kind of force of the illusion for its own sake, is not something one's terribly interested in.

That's why the magic tricks that I do always carry with them a narrative. There's a sequence of things that happen. Sometimes you can do things where things just vanish or appear which you then have to put into a narrative to make it meaningful. But generally the trick has within it a structure that you then have to find your own meaning for.

You know, you get the audience to take a card. The card gets lost and you say you're going to find it. You don't find the right card. It gets lost. Is it here? Is it here? Is it there? It's in the least expected place in the end and it's the same card, it's sealed away somewhere. This is almost an archetypal story. Which Freudians might say would have particular significance in terms of development. Is the card really the mother going away? Probably all those ideas are involved with many tricks. But the point is that it gives a **structure** to what you're doing.

And what happens if suddenly in the middle of a performance that structure falls apart and something goes wrong?

One of the things that I like about doing it is that within the structure you can create the **illusion** that things have gone wrong. And that's often part of the appeal of the magic trick. For one trick I borrow a ten-pound note like many magicians do and set fire to it accidentally and then I'm going to find it in a fruit but it's not there . . . And the whole process of acting a magician who's done it wrong, trying to actually work it so that the audience really does think it's gone wrong, is quite interesting as well. How do you actually do that? I think I do succeed with quite a large proportion of the audience.

Is part of the attraction of being a magician that of exerting a genuine power over the audience similar to the power which you suggest on stage?

The power to surprise people.

Like a before and after – take one sad person and turn them into a happy person after seeing the show.

Well, I suppose that's true of any performer, isn't it? It's not necessarily happy but changed. All the theatre I've been involved in I've wanted people to come out of it happier or changed. At the end of *Brecht on Magic* I get a note from Brecht, who has left me, saying: 'I told you at the end of your show people should leave the theatre and change the world. Well you're halfway there: they do leave the theatre.'

(Laughs.)

So, I think we all aspire to some change, some thought, however fleeting it may be, in the audience.

Maybe from the audience's point of view the idea of, the image of, the magician provides them with an example of that process which is essentially what they want to happen as well, that is: clear, swift, effortless and irreversible.

Yes, oh I think so, I think there's a sort of fairytale sort of appeal about magic as well – and there's the appeal of surprise and the appeal of things happening before your very eyes that you didn't possibly think could happen. I enjoy doing that.

I think the thing about magic is it forces you to do an open sort of style of theatre and even if you're doing ventriloquism as well, speaking to another character, it's still Brechtian in the sense that you are making a performance and it clearly *is* a performance. You don't get locked in the world that's created by those characters talking to one another. You also know that the audience is also on the lookout beforehand for the technicalities of this, is looking at it as a **process** rather than as a piece of reality being presented to them on a stage.

It's a way as well of extending your own discourse. It works very well in situations where there are things that you want to say or it's not quite the done thing to say or you're not quite allowed—

Well of course ventriloquists have always been portrayed by films as having these terrible split personalities, the dummy who murders the ventriloquist or whatever. You do see ventriloquist's dummies as a separate identity. I have sometimes been surprised by what the dummy has said to me. Because you're obviously using a different bit of your brain there to—

Is it difficult when the dummy starts to become the star of the show? There are only two of you there . . .

I've never experienced any pangs of jealousy about that, I must say. No, I don't think so. I think the dummy is almost bound to be the more compelling character. As a ventriloquist you take the pleasure that the audience gets from the dummy as your own and a lot of ventriloquists have always deliberately made the dummy a much stronger character than the ventriloquist.

There have been ventriloquists who **have** been – I think Edgar Bergen was a bit strange about his dummy, Charlie McCarthy. He had to have the original Charlie McCarthy. There was a time apparently when it got lost or had to be repaired so he had to use the spare and there's a story that somebody told about coming into the dressing room and seeing him looking at him and saying: 'When the real Charlie McCarthy comes back, you're going to be in trouble, the way you've been performing out there.' And his daughter, Candice Bergen, the actress, she talks about having had a very strange upbringing with this dummy.

So what sort of life do your dummies have off stage?

The two big dummies that I have of Bertolt Brecht and William Morris mostly are kept packed away. Occasionally I'll get them out and do a bit of practising with them, play around. I do use them actually because they're quite big, put them so that their backs are to the window in our front room.

As a burglar deterrent?

Yes. Anybody just glancing in thinks there's somebody sitting in there so whenever we go away we don't take them with us.

(Laughs.)

Of course they could get stolen.

Mm. Are you particular about letting other people touch them?

Only to the extent that other people do with props. I suppose I do feel like they have characters that I've created vested in them in a way. If other people use them it does seem a bit odd because the voice doesn't come out right. But I don't know, puppeteers are very protective of their puppets as well. It's another form of puppetry, isn't it? Mostly my family complains about just the mess of all the stuff that's around, not that I'm talking to them too much.

There was one ventriloquist who got a divorce and his wife cited the dummy as co-respondent – in America this was – and the court upheld it. When they had friends round he would get the dummy out and the dummy would say nasty things about the wife. That was deemed mental cruelty. But no, I don't have those problems.

nabil shaban
Acting is a drug

Nabil Shaban was born with Osteo Imperfecta (brittle bones)
and is confined to a wheelchair. He formed the Graeae
Theatre Company of disabled performers in 1980, touring
the UK, USA and Canada. He has played Hamlet, Jesus in
Godspell and Haile Selassie in Jonathan Miller's production
of *The Emperor* at the Royal Court Theatre and appeared in
Derek Jarman's film *Wittgenstein*. He has also written and
directed a variety of television projects.

What made you start performing? What drew you to it?

I think what drew me to it was fantasy, enactments of fantasy, opportunity to be things that I'm not normally. And as a child that was very strong. Probably all children like dressing up and playing games, pretending to be cowboys or knights or whatever – and I used to get a big kick out of that. I also used to entertain my friends by telling stories and invariably we'd want to act them out.

In a children's home, in a hospital, the only glimpse that you had of the outside world was through television. Television represented a very strange, bizarre world, a world where there was adventure, excitement, where you could be a hero, a heroine. And when you leave school, leave the institution, you find that generally life's not like that. You find that life is actually quite mundane and what you see on television bears very little resemblance to what you experience.

In a sense becoming an actor was an attempt to maintain that illusion, that desire to have an exciting life. If you can't have a really exciting life, if you can't be a genuine secret agent, at least you can be one in a play or a film – and you can be things that you don't normally get the freedom to be. So if you want to be a maniac, if you want to be a murderer, you can do it without having to go to prison. You can have sort of the experience without anyone really being killed and so on. For example, someone's asked me to play Caligula in Albert Camus's *Caligula* and I'm really excited about the prospect. Because I'm interested in history and a chance to dress up, Romans—

Togas!

Yeah, exactly. Living at a time when life was much rawer, when people behaved in a much more honest way. Life because of it was much more brutal. And just reading it I was getting a buzz, I could feel my blood rushing to my cheeks and I was thinking: I've really got to try and cultivate a madness so I could do it well. I have got to become insane for the period because then I feel that I can be effective, I can be believable.

And is that buzz something which tends to be more intense if you know there's a real possibility of doing the part or the play?

Oh yeah. It certainly happened reading Caligula – the more I think about it, the more excited I am by it. Someone mentioned Howard Barker's *Judith* with me playing the Assyrian general . . .

Holofernes.

Yeah. Because of my interest in death and battles and so on, it is something that's up my street. I like plays which really directly relate to my feelings, you know, the way I see the world.

And which do so in a very expressive and non-naturalistic way . . .

Story-telling is non-naturalistic. Although the setting is non-naturalistic, you'll try to make people believe that what they're seeing is natural – and that's the art, that's the skill involved. I'm going to be in a wheelchair when I play Caligula and there's going to be no attempt as far as I know to hide or disguise the chair. And I think it's important not to do that. Which will immediately make people think: Well, hang on, how can Caligula be in a wheelchair? What you have to do is you have to create a situation where it's not that they don't see the wheelchair, it's just that they don't **care** about the wheelchair being there or not.

Because what they're seeing is not representative of the historical facts of Caligula. If you read Tacitus or Suetonius or Robert Graves, they each come up with a different version. No one really knows what the truth is – and consequently you can use that and you can use the wheelchair to create a new truth. You can be a Caligula in or out of a wheelchair, that's the point.

And it's exactly what all actors do with themselves and the circumstances of their being, their bodies – it just so happens you have a wheelchair on stage with you.

You can be a hero or a tyrant whether you're disabled or not.

I think that's quite clear, certainly from all your performances that I've seen, there's never been any problem with that.

In a film which tries to be realistic in terms of shooting and natural locations I think it can be jarring to present someone in a wheelchair. So if you did a movie version of *Caligula*, it would have to be done by someone like Jarman or Greenaway, who would use stylistic techniques to make it more of an abstract piece.

They're both directors who have specialised in looking very clearly at the reality of the illusion.

Yeah. Yeah.

And that's what you get every time you go into the theatre. Also I think through the increasing popularity of things like video and the fact that far more people now can make their own videos, people are beginning to trust that medium more to do those sort of things. Which is good, which is what I think they are there for – to let you be Caligula if you want to be.
   Maybe having talked about what you get out of it, we could talk a bit about audiences. What are your experiences with them?

I think it's very difficult for actors to know what's going on with the audiences. Sometimes you come off stage and think: 'God, they're a terrible audience, you really had to work hard with them' – and another actor will say: 'No, no, I don't agree, I think they were a very intelligent audience, they were just listening intently.' Different actors can have different interpretations on any one night as to what the audience's reaction is. An audience member may come up to you after the show, but no one's ever had the courage to say: 'I thought you were terrible, I thought it was crap what you did.' They always say: 'Oh that was really nice' or: 'I loved that.' So you never get a **real** feeling.
   If people come to the next night, and the next night – if you're playing to full houses – then there's possibly a good chance that generally it's been well received. But there again that needn't necessarily be the case, it might be

that it's just hip to go to the show. When we were doing *The Emperor* upstairs at the Court there seemed to be more stars in the audience than on stage. At the end of the show or in the interval we would say: Who's out there tonight? James Baldwin's out there tonight, oh wow! Arthur Miller, wowee! Faye Dunaway – ah shit, man! . . . You almost had the feeling that the audiences were coming because it was a kind of social occasion.

And in a way, as a disabled actor, it's even stranger, I think, because there was a time when I first started when I kept thinking: They only think I'm good because I'm disabled. Because they've got no yardstick: they've never seen someone in a wheelchair do this sort of performing before, so whatever I do's going to look good. In the end it always comes down to whether you get offered another job, then you know that obviously someone thinks that you're worth enough to actually fork out some money to pay you. That is what finally tells you whether you're an actor or not.

You **can** tell for yourself, if when you've done something or when you're doing it you can get a great buzz out of it. You know if your face is like burning. Obviously you're not going to get that night after night. It's really hard, it's so depressing when you can't recapture it. The killer is when you consciously **try** to do it. You had it last night and you think: God, I hope I can get it tonight! The moment you think of doing that, then you lose it. So you've got to try and enter every performance afresh, like it's the first time you've ever done it in your life. Then you stand a chance of **perhaps** recapturing that quality that you may have got, that one special night when you really felt you could sense the audience. For that moment then, you **do** sense them. The audience has been taken somewhere else and they really sense what you are telling them – and are frightened or moved or really believe in the love affair that's going on or whatever. When you can achieve that it's like a mystical experience in a way.

I've got a friend who says, for her, acting is a drug. And in many ways it **is** a drug, you want to achieve a high from it. I'd recommend it to anyone – I wouldn't want anybody off acting. I think it's a great experience and you can learn, you can reach such heights with discovering the insides of yourself, of your mind.

The other great thing about working in this profession is that there's a lot of knowledge to be gained. So for example doing *The Emperor*, you're not just doing the play, you're actually learning about Ethiopia and you're learning about Ethiopia in the context of Africa and Ethiopia during the war and also you start to learn about Rastafarianism because you know that Haile Selassie is blah blah blah. And doing a play about Caligula, you then suddenly learn everything you can and try to study about Roman history and so on. And there aren't that many jobs, really, where you get the opportunity to be able to almost learn an entire new subject every time you do a piece of work.

You're taking things which on the surface would appear extremely distant and making them very real and very tangible, looking at them on very personal levels. How does this person behave in a particular situation? What is it like to be in the same room as them? What are the emotions which are going on within this person at a particular moment? Do I also feel these things sometimes? There is a continuous search in creating theatre, which I think is extremely rewarding – and something that again, once you've got a taste for it, it's very difficult to stop. Afterwards, when you come off, you're not just going to go home, go to bed and fall asleep.

Right. I don't drink now but I used to, up until about '82. I started acting in 1980 and once I started performing, I found I was drinking more and more, particularly after the show. Because you have all this adrenalin being pumped around you and you can reach such heights, you want to come back down at the end of the show. So I'd be drinking vodka or gin or whatever and it's a very social thing anyway. Most theatres have a bar and you know you can't very well just piss off . . . And I suddenly had to stop myself and I thought: My God, I know **now** why Peter O'Toole and Richard Burton, whoever, ad infinitum, ended up the way they did. Because the drug leads on to the other drug. Because you're using the drug adrenalin, you'll end up having to need others. So I consciously stopped drinking in '82 – but I'm kind of lucky that I live out of London, which means that I drive home after a show. I've got about forty miles to drive, so I can come back down by driving very fast, listening to rock'n'roll, very loud, down the A3, at night, which is a great way of coming down off the adrenalin drug.

So anyone being overtaken at high speed—

They'll know that I've just done a show, yeah. And they can hear the Sex Pistols or whatever coming blaring out.

We were talking on the phone and you described how much you like being in the country. Yet theatres always seem to be in very noisy, crowded areas and in cities: is that an attraction or does it put you off?

I hate the crowds. I really hate being amongst crowds. It's quite odd because on stage you're not part of the crowd any more, you've almost got splendid isolation. So long as I can't see the audience, I don't feel bad. So the lights need to be nice and strong, so they black everything else out, and I don't wear my glasses.

I've got so many ambivalent attitudes towards being an actor and performing, the whole business of acting. Often in the wings waiting to come on, I'm sort of thinking: Why am I doing this? What's this play going to do to help change the world? Has it really got such a profound story that people need to know it? Why am I doing it? Am I an egotist? Am I going on stage because I want everyone to sort of look up at me and think, wow! I'm shit scared, quaking like mad – and going through torture. This happens nearly every first night.

Another thought that often happens as I'm waiting in the wings is: I'd really like to go out on stage now, get my cock out and piss in front of everybody – just because it's a totally meaningless act which is aimed to shock, it's a desire to change all the rules. People would come in to expect to see a play and instead someone comes on, does an obscene act, gets fired and is never seen again. There's almost a self-destruct element to me with respect to acting. I have to keep telling myself: Well, there are reasons. As a disabled person you have an obligation to be an actor, because there aren't many disabled people working in theatre, film and television. Because of that, most disabled people feel excluded from the everyday world. They don't see themselves represented, they don't see themselves as having families, as having jobs, being fathers, being daughters, being in love, hating, fighting, whatever – doing something that's contributing to society at all. And since I've managed to get in somehow, I have a responsibility to try to feature as much as possible, presenting images of a disabled person in lots of different situations, so that both the able-bodied public and the disabled public can start to have different attitudes about disabled people. That is the one thing that keeps me thinking that it's worthwhile being an actor.

But you're not saying if it wasn't for this obligation you wouldn't carry on acting?

Possibly. I'd probably do it for a short while because that's why I have this ambivalent attitude about it, I'm not quite sure. I sort of think: Well, there are other more worthwhile things to be doing in a way in the world and why be an actor? What is worthwhile about that profession? Apart from if you genuinely want to be involved in story-telling and you want to be involved in presenting mirrors to society, then that's a good enough reason to be an actor – to be involved in things which are reminding people about who they are and where they're going and what they should be striving for. Any other reason seems to be purely selfish and those reasons don't interest me.

I wonder whether that means that able-bodied people don't have any reason to be actors, taking it to its logical—

Yeah, right!

I was going to do a PhD once on the psychology of entertainment and I was going to look just specifically at comedy. I tortured myself for about two weeks and watched every comedy programme that the four channels were churning out. They were dire. It put me off. I decided I didn't want to be able to discover the secret of what makes people laugh – because if I did that, then it might end up producing even more dire comedies.

But I am interested in the psychology of entertainment, the need for entertainment. I think there are certain basic needs that a human being has. The obvious ones are food, shelter, sex and entertainment. And you'll find that no matter where you go in the world at whatever time in man's history.

Do you think we've reached a stage now where we live with a surfeit of entertainment?

I'm only entertained if I'm made to think or if I'm encouraged to experience something which I wouldn't normally experience or if I'm being made to question things. So I've got a very limited range of things that I will watch because of that. Television is getting worse and worse – and I think it's kind of deliberate on the part of the ruling elite. Because they don't believe in real democracy and to have real democracy you've got to have an educated mass of people and that's the one thing they don't want.

On the other hand, if you then have the opportunity to do what you believe in, isn't there then an obligation to do it?

If the opportunities come, then I'll take them. But I fear that those opportunities are getting less and less – or you try and create them.

I think this is the crucial question because it's this ability to create opportunity which is something which I think a lot of actors find especially difficult.

You see, I **had** to create the opportunity for me to become an actor. Because I wasn't going to be accepted as an actor by the mainstream or even by the local am dram societies. You know, when I got in touch with my local am dram, they were just going to give me scenery-painting jobs or prompting, they didn't consider me as being a possible actor. And drama schools weren't interested.

So in a sense because I'd had that experience of having to create the opportunity in the first place by setting up a theatre company of disabled actors, I suppose I'm more used to the idea that as an actor I have to have an active part in trying to get myself work. That leads me into being a writer and leads me into being a producer. Because I know that the opportunities are going to get few and far between if I just sit around and wait for my agent to ring me and tell me something's happening.

And the company you formed is Graeae.

Yeah. And they've always had a very specific disability message. A few years ago they did a play about gay disabilities. Last year they did a piece based on Albie Sachs, because he lost his arm when South African secret terror squads blew up his car. It was quite an interesting approach to that because they had two actors playing Albie Sachs, a black actor and then a guy who was white but he didn't have an arm. Three years ago they did a play about blind people and their experiences of guide dogs and charities and all of that. So they've always been polemical. I think they're going to be here to stay.

When we set up Graeae, we hoped several things. That we would spawn lots of theatre companies around the country, and then secondly that we would change the mainstream theatrical profession to such a degree that maybe Graeae and companies like Graeae would no longer be needed. So we kind of had the idea of a self-destruct button being built into it.

Having said that, if it hasn't ceased to exist that's not necessarily a failure. Theatre companies are groups of people who like working together, who because of the collective experience have become better at working with each other than with other people. Then that company is the logical place for them to continue.

Sure. I mean the only failure would be if they exist because mainstream theatre was still acting prejudicially towards disabled performers. But I don't think that will be the ultimate reason why Graeae will continue to exist. It will be because there are groups of people who have these shared experiences which they want to be able to present and this is the best forum for doing it.

sue lefton &
gerald wooster
Dr Theatre

Sue Lefton is a director and movement director. She has worked with Adrian Noble, Mike Alfreds, Declan Donellan, Max Stafford-Clark, Deborah Warner, Roman Polanski and many others. Recent productions as director include *A Doll's House* and *Miss Julie* at the New End Theatre, London. Dr Gerald Wooster is a retired consultant psychotherapist at St George's Hospital, London, and an associate member of the British Psychoanalytical Society. He has a special interest in the relationship between psychotherapy and the theatre.

SUE LEFTON: Gerald is the most dedicated theatregoer I know. He sees far more than anyone who works in the theatre.

GERALD WOOSTER: Why do you think people go to the theatre?

I can only speak from personal experience. I suppose the initial attraction, when I was growing up, was that it was a chance to observe what the world was like when I wasn't part of it. The theatre seemed a terribly valuable source of information about what other people were actually like. In a way it was a sort of licensed voyeurism.

GW: That's interesting, because there are some similarities with our work here at the Group Analytical Practice. In a group you are seeing and hearing how the other people are living their lives, you can compare your own life with their side of things more openly. I suppose it links up with two other forms of treatment, dramatherapy and psychodrama.

Dramatherapy is listening to a very meaningful story or myth and then the dramatherapist seeks to see how the people in the group are working and relating to that story. Psychodrama is a technique where often people take turns to present themselves as the protagonist in centre stage and act through some formative experience that happened to them. The other people in the group assume the roles of the other participants and afterwards they may give their experience back to the protagonist: what it must have felt like to be them and what they felt about the situation the protagonist was in. They give them some extremely valuable feedback.

SL: These things are where people are observing but would then *be* the theatre. The audience become protagonists themselves – if not in that session, then in another one. In the theatre the actors are **always** the actors. An audience is not going to switch around and be acting next.

Actors are very unaware about the nature of an audience. They can feel an audience is penetrating, persecuting and potentially damaging. Whereas when you're in a group you might feel a little nervous about revealing yourself but very quickly you're made to feel an equal. Other people make connections and identifications with you very openly, so everybody sort of empathises with each other. I think that distance between the audience and the actor and the **strangeness**, the other of the audience for the actor, has detrimental effects both on the performance and on the audience – and therefore has detrimental effects on the interaction between them. The potential for theatre has to live between those two. And I think that's something we are trying to explore in a particular kind of way.

I think though in balance to what you said about the performer's feelings of persecution, the audience like being able to see performers performing for them. And while for a performer there is always an element of danger in appearing before an audience, if the audience weren't there they wouldn't be doing it.

SL: Actors do **long** for an audience but it's very ambivalent. My sense of it is that they want an audience but they're very, very afraid and that that somehow doesn't allow them to rest in their parts, with their minds focussed on the issues in the play. There's this clamouring, this wanting to be watched . . . It's very complicated, often it's in competition with the other actors on stage regardless of the meaning of the play.

From my experiences it's remarkable how little one sees of that, those sort of competitive feelings, either in the performance or in the creative process. My personal feeling is that actors as a group of people are extremely pleasant and sociable to be with and to work with – more so than any other professional group I've ever encountered.

GW: For all its difficulties, that people can express themselves and different parts of themselves on the stage is in fact good for the development of those people. Obviously there's a mixed bag. It's interesting perhaps the sort of more pathological end of why people choose acting.

SL: I don't want to exaggerate because I know actors who need and feel at home on the stage, there are many different types of people. But I think that there is something which isn't really looked at, which is that the audience is left a little bit as a stranger not to be discussed, rather like you don't discuss death or you don't discuss age. You say: Oh, they're a bit slow tonight or: They're fantastic tonight, or: They're warming up. There's not much investigation. I think it would be fascinating to pursue some of these questions: Why is that audience warming to me, what's enabled it to happen? What is the two-way process?

I think it's very interesting to be having this discussion in England because I tend to find that English audiences' range of response is actually quite narrow compared with audiences in some other countries.

sl: Well, that's really what I'm saying. Audiences are very strange to us in this country and therefore they remain a little bit frightening.

I've talked to people who work on the comedy circuit who say that the range of audience response there is much broader and that this increases the anxieties that they have about performing.

sl: Comedy is always more frightening than tragedy to play in because I think performers have some idea that they're disliked if they're not laughed at, that they're failing. So they become a bit depressed and consequently the audience **can't** laugh, because a person who's depressed in the wrong kind of way can't make you laugh. It's a very strong interaction, albeit a negative one. Likewise when an actor goes out and just happens to get the audience, the next actor is liked a little bit more because of that and the whole thing takes off.

I don't think actors really know how much power they have over the audience – to provoke their imaginations, how impressed they are with them and how marvellous they think they are to even do it, let alone to be fantastically brilliant all the time. And what isn't available to actors because of their anxiety about an audience is that an audience comes full of their own lives, full of their own interpretations, full of their own projections onto the play. And they are capable of enjoying it because of what they are themselves – not necessarily always because of what an actor or a director's done but because of the fullness of their lives and their insights. Actors often feel so **responsible** whether these people have a good evening. And up to a point it's up to the people themselves. This is a very important thing. If actors could cease to be so anxious about meeting their audiences, they might begin to see that the responsibility doesn't all lie with them, that if there was the odd moment that wasn't that great, nobody's going to tear them apart.

gw: I suppose this venture we've been involved in has been aiding and abetting that coming together. We've had one or two people doing talks, responding to the theatre profession or the literary profession from a psychoanalytic view. And each time actors and actresses came in after their performance and commented from their experience on playing parts we had just seen, that was the most exciting part of the exercise. The format that has been particularly nice has been the one with your production of *A Doll's House* in a small theatre, where you have a break and then come back into the auditorium and the performers are on stage and they can ask questions of the audience and vice versa.

sl: There's a lot an audience has to say, there's a lot of energy that's been building up. They've been sitting there for two or three hours and they've been working too. Somehow they're all tuned to the same event. And there was something very touching about the audience because none of them tried to be clever. Nobody was being madly academic and making marvellously interesting points. It was quite simple and heart-felt and rather straight-forwardly communicated and the actors were responding in the same kind of way. It was a very immediate kind of event for everybody and they felt they had their say and it didn't go on too long.

And the actors – maybe I'm dreaming, maybe I'm mad – but the actors' performances were better for it the next night. The issues that had been brought up the night before had become subtler and there was a much more palpable involvement. Which was very helpful for us. It was very mutually creative.

Do you think it's only a small proportion of the audience who would be interested in seeing a performance and then returning for a discussion afterwards?

sl: Probably, yes. You're not going to get everybody who goes to the theatre wanting to come and discuss. A lot of people do not want to do that at all. But then that may well be the kind of theatre that I'm not so very interested in. I can't imagine people coming back later to discuss – well, maybe they **would** start discussing *Miss Saigon* . . . Maybe there are different sorts of discussions for different sorts of theatre. It's an interesting question you asked, would this be a narrower audience, because I rather sort of snobbishly said yes but now I think no. No. You *could* get the most fantastic—

It strikes me that what you're interested in doing is a kind of performance which is a process rather than an event.

GW: Yes, and I think that there's a parallel process worth mentioning. There are two bestsellers amongst our profession, books by Joyce McDougall called *The Theatres of the Body* and *The Theatres of the Mind*, really encouraging us to look at our work in terms of the theatre as metaphor. That the body is reacting, giving messages, it communicates in images that are often highly conflictual.

Theatre has traditionally explored very highly charged human situations and has represented rather extreme cases of human behaviour and I wonder what the obligation to make this as convincing as possible entails for the performer.

I'm interested in whether the anxieties that Sue talked about are in a way necessary to the process, whether they are also what gives the actors then the power that you describe them having over an audience, whether those things go together.

GW: It's **very** interesting what you're bringing up.

SL: I know various people have become very depressed by playing Hamlet. And I think that really does happen. I think that the part does that to the actor in quite a deep sense. They enter into the pathology, almost, of the character.

GW: It would make sense because a lot of the actual techniques are to do with mirroring. I'm more and more finding in my work looking at mirroring how much we are seeing signs of ourselves through other people. There is a brilliant piece of stagecraft from Ibsen, which I saw recently in *The Lady from the Sea*, where one triangle among the subsidiary characters mirrors and opens up the chief triangle of Ellida, her husband, and the stranger who is trying to seduce her away. And there must be times where if you find yourself called on to play a very powerful part which has lots of quite loud resonances with your own experience, if you're sensitive or finely-tuned, as it were, it's likely to come out one way or another. And it's part of the work, of course, in our profession – we have to watch and look for what gets at us and try and use this not just as a damn nuisance but as a valuable area of sensitivity to employ.

SL: So you mean a patient may actually make you angry?

GW: Yes.

SL: Which, if you can overcome that and analyse and understand it, you might be able to use creatively rather than just getting in a bad temper and waiting for them to go.

GW: Yes, that's right.

SL: It's the same with an actor if the character really gets to them. I certainly think all these things we've said this afternoon, when I talk about anxieties and stress, I do see it as a potential for being **creative**, not a potential for being negative.

Is it worth knowing what those nerves are? What that means? What creates those nerves? Is it the same every time or do the nerves have a different quality to them according to what play they're doing?

The strongest attraction that theatre has for me now is of a world which is different from the world that exists. That the character is not the actor. Oddly enough, my experience of actors playing Hamlet has not been of people who took on all the psychological problems going on within that character. The actors I knew playing that part loved doing so.

SL: Mine is really different. And I'm sure there's truth in both.

Though I can see the intellectual temptation – the idea of all these things matching up and Hamlet becoming insane is quite an appealing one – my gut feeling about the theatre and why I love it suggests also there is a very strong force in the other direction. Of people getting on with the show despite all kinds of personal tragedy. So there are those two conflicting impulses at work simultaneously.

GW: Have you experiences of what this is like?

SL: Dr Theatre, it's called. Certainly it seems to supply a way of denying, avoiding the experience. If during the day you've just found out you've got the most terrible disease or something has happened to someone you love, you can suspend that thought when you're on a stage and for those two or three hours completely lose yourself in your performance in a way that I can't imagine you could do in any other place.

I personally had an experience when I couldn't walk, I had such a bad back that I was unable to put any weight on my right leg, I thought I would limp through the performance at a hop. And the moment I put my foot on the stage the pain was gone. The moment I came off again, I couldn't move. It is an extraordinary mind-over-matter thing that happens to people. It has enormous power, over all sorts of things.

katrin cartlidge
Touching more nerves

Katrin Cartlidge was a member of the acting company for the
National Theatre Studio's Festival of New Plays in the
Cottesloe Theatre, directed by Peter Gill and John Burgess.
She has been involved in a wide variety of new work both at
the Studio – where this interview took place – and
elsewhere, including plays by Jonathan Moore, Chris
Hannan, Nick Ward, David Edgar and Gregory Motton and
Steven Berkoff's productions of *Salomé* and *The Trial*. She
was awarded Most Promising European Actress at the
Geneva Film Festival for her performance in Mike Leigh's
Naked and also appears in *Before The Rain*, winner of the
Golden Lion at the 1994 Venice Film Festival

Acting in theatre one gets the opportunity to have a kind of delicious amnesia and to go on each night pretending one's never done it before, yet having the experience of having done so. You've got a continual *Dog Day Afternoon* situation where the events never change but the subtleties, chemistry and magic can.

What about theatres as places? Do you think they're nice places to be?

I think we've lost touch with theatres as places, really, in terms of how we define them, because they're either these tiny little spaces or vast spaces. And I think we don't recognise that they're two completely separate forms of theatre. Very often we transfer things from small spaces into big spaces, which is nonsense, really. All too often people don't rethink the show and so they rattle around in big theatres when the show was designed for a small one. Or people are forced to work in small venues when really they need the width and space of a big one – and that's to do with economics. The epic modern play is almost extinct as a result. Because nobody is going to take the financial risk of putting on or encouraging a new writer and director to create for a big space with a large cast. That limits the experimental large work to subsidised theatres – and very often subsidised theatres won't take the risk now either.

The contemporary epic is in trouble in lots of ways because also our lives are getting less and less epic in that we experience things in a very claustrophobic manner. We are more and more encouraged to stay in our little boxes with computers, televisions, telephones, faxes – our lives are becoming less spatially orientated, which is ironic in this age of travel.

I think what you're talking about is the breadth of an experience and I think that there are people around who are capable of using the theatre to analyse as it were the depth of a particular experience or set of experiences. And I think that is actually what theatre is good at.

Well, hopefully it's a combination of those things. But it's so rare that people are given an opportunity to do it. The whole notion of how to relate to a space and to a theatre is becoming smaller and smaller and smaller. I feel sad about that.

When you watch, say, Robert Lepage's *Tectonic Plates*, that definitely had a breadth because of the way that he used the Cottesloe. The traverse space was very important because he was trying to express intercontinental and international situations. It was very important to have a wide space between people and to travel between countries and cultures – and to have water and different **elements**. That's what I mean by filling a space: it's elemental as well as spatial. And people like him can do it because their experience is not limited to a particular country, which is very interesting. I think as soon as you get out of being in a particular country, you have a much greater canvas to draw on.

Having said that, in London especially, there is such a huge racial and ethnic mix around that you would have thought it would be quite possible to integrate all that.

I think it is. I think it's the way it has to go. But it's surprising how much resistance there is to it.

Théâtre de Complicité are obvious exceptions to all this. They are devoted to a mixture of culture and race in their work. But apart from them, there is a lack of ensembles in British theatre which is detrimental to the artistic development of individual actors. If you never get a chance to play your range as an actor, it's like having a voice that you can't practise with, you can't hit the high notes or the low notes. You need to push yourself in several different directions in order that one may inform the other. And it's essential to push your own boundaries further and further apart.

This doesn't happen because people get typecast. Even in theatre. And there isn't an ensemble situation where somebody who might be playing a small role in one play could be doing the lead in the next. We don't have that system here. So there are muscles which the actors in Britain don't ever get to develop and that makes them unfit, if you know what I mean, in terms of their craft.

So what can they do to flex these muscles?

There's very little you can do as an actor unless you're given the opportunity. It's the old cliché: as a painter you can paint, as a writer you can write, as a dancer you can dance, but as an actor you cannot act without being given the opportunity. That's why it's tragic. It's a real artistic deprivation, not to encourage and take risks with actors who need to explore their range.

I think range tends to happen in terms of media. Sometimes the people involved in one medium don't have the preconceptions of people involved in another. I'm amazed, to be honest, at the versatility that it's possible to achieve for example in film. I assumed that typecasting would be much more the case than it is in theatre. Currently I'm finding that I'm being offered a much wider range of parts in film, almost than I am in the theatre, which is bizarre. There are more casting risks being taken in certain types of film than in the theatre! Considering the budgets involved and considering that if you fuck a film up nobody is going to give you another chance, you'd think they'd be playing it safe as houses, but they're not. Obviously they could get more risky, much more risky, but it's interesting all the same.

I did a new play by Gregory Motton at the Royal Court Theatre not that long ago and it ran for **two** weeks. The rehearsal period was four. I don't understand that. It's so lacking in faith. We sold out for most of the run – but the two weeks had been decided before rehearsals began! And that's supposed to be the 'risky' end of the Fringe. So it's pretty appalling really. That's the kind of attitude that is preventing the growth of a potentially fertile medium. I think it really is stifling. I mean how many playwrights of my generation are there? How many are regularly seen in the London theatres?

The fact is that they tend to get very few productions. But there are lots of people around writing.

Well, **I** don't know about them. I've never heard of them. And I'm an actor.

You've done a lot of new plays!

But I could probably count them all on my two hands, I can count the writers I've done on my two hands in fourteen years of acting. Now I can't believe that's all there are so where are all these people? **Where** are they being blocked? **Why** are they being blocked? And **who** is blocking them?

There's a certain minimum requirement which isn't being attended to in this country at the moment, and if you don't attend to it, we will just lose that generation. It's as simple as that. We will lose a whole generation of performers and writers because they won't have an outlet for their voice and therefore no one can hear them. Because there's no such thing as creating a play in your attic. It won't be found with dust on it in fifty years' time.

This has happened with writers like Büchner.

I agree. But there's nothing like a production of a writer's play, particularly if it's a contemporary play performed in the society in which it is set by actors who belong to that society. And if it isn't financed or it isn't done or no one risks it, then that's it, it's wasted.

Does working with a new play, something that hasn't been seen before, something that's maybe still being rewritten as you're rehearsing it, where you don't know what's going to come out at the end – is that a different process to working on a known text?

It's much more frightening, more unnerving, actually. Very often new plays, particularly if they're good, tread an unsettling line between what you think you know and what you actually haven't learned yet.

About the play?

About life. Whatever it's looking at. And often it takes the entire run before you really, really understand it, I find. If it's good. I'm lucky inasmuch as I think nearly all the new plays I've done have been like that. I'd much rather do a new play and run the risk of it not working at all, particularly if there's something in it that is interesting and I want to know more about. A lot of people seem to be more interested in re-examining territory already trodden than they are in watching or being with a new piece of work which is unpredictable. There's no other word to describe it. It is unpredictable.

And does this carry a greater responsibility with it as well, for the actor?

I like that challenge. I really like it. It's harder to win an audience over to a new piece of work because they find it unsettling. They don't know what to expect. They can't sit back and go: Oh, yes, they've done it like that, I see. There's something about the way a contemporary piece can touch on nerves which no other piece can.

I suppose as well there's a greater chance of someone coming along and thinking you actually are the character.

Or they don't want to accept the character at all. The experience of playing Sophie in *Naked* has been quite, quite phenomenal. The whole notion of that character created so many problems for people watching it: **Are** there people like that? Am I like that? Is there any aspect of me that's like that? Have I ever seen anyone like that?

Another thing which comes into it – perhaps less with that character but certainly with other characters in contemporary films – is: I want to be like that.

They certainly didn't want to be like her! And that's what upset them as well – they want to feel: I want to be like that. And when they're presented with somebody who reminds them of aspects of themselves they would really rather forget and certainly dissociate themselves from, then they're very disturbed indeed and that happens a lot in contemporary work across the board, whatever it is.

When you're right on top of a contemporary situation, just the proximity of it makes it difficult to view it objectively and people get much more upset. Their range of interpretation of a modern piece, I notice, is so vast, depending on who they are and what their lives are like, much more than on a historical piece. When I did Nick Ward's play *Apart from George* in which the girl I played, Linda, had been abused by her father, there were certain people who could not understand why the character was so horrible to her father. They were totally blind to the fact of the abuse. Then there were others who understood straight away – and this was fascinating. Some things are very visible in a modern piece to some people and completely invisible to others, depending on their perspective.

I think that's one of the real things that a live theatre piece can do which other media can't achieve nearly so well, present a situation in which you communicate to people that something is happening without actually showing them directly. And exploring through a number of performances the way that various people pick up on that and various other people don't but still can actually enjoy the performance and piece together a world there, is very interesting.

That is fantastic. Film's much more like writing a letter because the people will get it months later and you don't know how they're going to interpret it when they read it. Theatre is a conversation. It's a conversation between the actors and the writer but mainly a conversation between the actors and the audience. If the actor isn't communicating to the audience, it doesn't matter what the writer's written, it won't be heard.

Often in performances when you don't listen, it's not because what's written isn't vital but because the way it's being said isn't vital. I personally love the intimacy of a small theatre for that conversation, I think I'm better at the intimacy, I'm unskilled in big theatre communication because I've not had much opportunity, basically. It would take me quite a long time to adjust to a big space. Working with Steven Berkoff was great from that point of view. Because I felt that he really does have the language of the big space at his fingertips and he knows how to communicate – so it was very, very informative to be able to work with him.

Could he communicate that to the actors he was working with?

If by no other way, by doing it and by us watching **him** do it every night.

Is that something you would rather do, you would rather watch your colleagues than be told to do something in a particular way?

Well it's interesting actually because Steven is a visual person, although he's very articulate and he can write reams for the *Guardian* and all sorts – hello, Steven! – but sometimes he would actually do whatever it was he wanted you to do. And when this happened it was not that he expected you to do exactly the same, but it was his way of describing in a total form. Like an apprentice might be shown how to make a hammer.

It's simply the most effective means of communication.

Yes. And there's been a big sort of: Oh no, you must never show an actor exactly what to do! But the only reason Steven can do it is because he **is** an actor. It wouldn't work if he was purely a director who couldn't act his way out of a paper bag because that would be very distracting. But it's interesting that Steven can do it just by showing you in the way a craftsman would show you how to do something, and I enjoyed that. Because it's a much more organic way of learning something. It goes without saying that Steven has the ability to inspire, which also goes beyond craft.

Actors have to be very broadminded in terms of how they work. They can't afford to be like writers and directors, people who are much lonelier in their role. An actor needs variety. I would loathe just to do one type of thing the whole time. It would drive me nuts.

To go from the working method of, say, Steven Berkoff to the working method of Mike Leigh, you find that one definitely informs the other. As an actor it's a joy to have that extremity of experience.

What about Mike Leigh? What about his way of creating characters and creating the story with them?

That is a life experience, really. To have the opportunity to use your skill, your observations of humanity and character, which are your main staples as an actor, to inform the narrative nature of a piece, is a most thrilling combination. I'm not even talking about results, just to go on that journey with somebody as skilled as Mike is, was so exhilarating and stimulating and fascinating and psychologically informative – it is actually a sort of journey of self-discovery as well. Because your imagination starts to work on a level that it's never been given the freedom to do before.

Can you describe a bit more fully the way this process works?

I can, I'll try to, but it becomes increasingly more difficult because when you're working with Mike you only ever see the process from your perspective.

Your character's perspective?

No, the actor's perspective. Basically you start off just with Mike, building a character, and then he puts you into improvisations with other actors who are at the same stage. You are never allowed to discuss, outside of those improvisations, anything that's gone on within them – either with other actors or with anyone else. That's an extraordinary experience in itself, just to feel all these things going on in your head that you can't get out.

It was a positive experience in fact – because I discovered that there are an awful lot of problems you get as an actor that if you talk about them, simply become ten times worse. Whereas if you just shut up and allow yourself to think it through, there's a natural process for working things out which happens.

I can imagine it being very difficult if you've got a serious problem.

People were watching me going through something that I couldn't express. I couldn't come home and express what I'd been through the day that Sophie was raped by the landlord and I couldn't exactly come home whistling either. There were times when it really was quite awful not being able to talk about it, but at the same time it was a very interesting aspect of working with him. I'd like to think that I've carried some of that with me into other things I've done. Now I don't always go into great detail telling people what I'm doing, I just say: I don't talk about it till it's finished. Because it helps, I find, to keep you in that world, in the world of film, in the world of the play. I quite like that.

Anyway, for four months you do these explorations and improvising in which anything could happen, quite literally, and from that Mike decides which aspects he most wants to explore further in the film. He makes a structure of scenes and you only know what happens in the scenes you are involved in.

And so do you then film them in chronological order?

Yes. As much as is humanly possible. Because when you come to film you re-examine some of those aspects. For example, you might re-examine where Sophie met Johnny on the steps. That's all the heading would be. And then you'd come to reimprovise that scene without any pressure to repeat anything. That would then be honed down until it was right, whatever it was, until Mike had agreed that that was the right scene and you agreed that that's what you would say – and then it gets filmed. Ideally it has to be chronological because something might change from before that might affect the next scene. So he can't really film out of sequence.

This is a really simplistic way of describing how Mike works and actually he's fed up of describing how he works because it's so open to misinterpretation, so open to misunderstanding. I'm always quite nervous about doing it. I think it's a great method actually; really, really wonderful. Particularly because in film you are wanting to create the atmosphere where something elusive can happen and the less the person knows about what is going to happen to them, the less they can predetermine how they're going to behave, the more likely you'll catch that elusivity.

In theatre the challenge is to create the **illusion** of elusivity and actually re-examine the nature of what that is so that you come each night to retread the same structural ground and still be spontaneous. That is an extraordinary challenge too. I think the best moments that I've had in the theatre as an actor have been almost close to trance-like situations. By that I don't mean out of my head, but I have let go or I have trusted the conscious aspect of my being to support the inspirational aspect. There is something quite special that can happen in a performance that feels almost chemical. It's not conscious. You have your conscious apparatus to fall back on if you can't breathe but actually the moments that work best for me are the moments where you leave that consciousness behind and there's a sort of timelessness. It's like getting lost in anything, it's the moment you get lost in sex and suddenly don't realise that you've been at it for hours, it's that same thing. It's leaving the constraints of one's consciousness, actually. And that's hard. It's really hard to trust yourself to do it. And it's something to do with going into one's imagination.

I do believe there are other ways, **apart** from technique, of communicat-ing with people – just like there are in life. Being in love with someone is not a technique. It's a genuine emotion. And I think as an actor there are moments when you are performing when the reality of the emotion you are feeling goes beyond your technique. They're not moments you can press buttons to create. You can press buttons to create other things in the **hope** that that will happen, but it's those moments which for me are essentially theatrical and they're between you and the audience and they're what make a piece of theatre. And I know when I'm watching that. I know I can see it when an actor does it and so can everyone – I can see it, feel it, when an actor's prepared to do that.

I think to have a skill which allows you to lose your self-consciousness is for me the ultimate aim. I worked with a Yugoslavian actor, Rade Serbedzija, on *Before the Rain*, who's done forty films and I said to him: This is my second, please can you tell me something, give me some advice? And he said: I don't know when it happened, but maybe after twenty films, one day I just forgot the camera. I don't know why, but I forgot it. Yet watching him, he was so accurate technically, he knew exactly what he'd done for continuity. I could see, I knew, that he was deeply aware of the camera, but at the same time totally unaware of it. To be able to achieve that combination as a performer is what I think is sublime.